SHATTERED
PIECES,
LOVING
HEART

SHATTERED PIECES, LOVING HEART

MICHELE SANDOVAL POITRAS

Outskirts Press, Inc.
Denver, Colorado

Outskirts Press, Inc.
http://www.outskirtspress.com

ISBN: 978-1-4327-6818-8

Outskirts Press and the "OP" logo are trademarks belonging to Outskirts Press, Inc.

Dedication

To Tina, Jeremy and Shawna: *I believe the closest I will ever come to perfection in my life is when I brought each of you into this world. I carried you next to my heart for nine months, held you when you took your first breath, watched you stumble with your first steps and dried your tears when you cried. I know it has not always been easy at times having me for a mom throughout the years, but I also know that you are aware of how very much I love you. My wish has always been that the three of you would accomplish more I have been able to in my lifetime, and each of you has succeeded far beyond what I could imagine. From the words of the song I used to sing to you at bedtime before you closed your little eyes each night: "Dreams really do come true." All my love always, Mom*

Table of Contents

Foreword

- *I have tried to recreate events, locales, and conversations from my memories of them. In order to maintain their anonymity in some instances I have changed the names of individuals and places, I may have changed some identifying characteristics and details such as physical properties, occupations, and places of residence.*

I wish I could say I had an epiphany, and the pain, sorrow, fears, and insecurities in my life had vanished. Well in my world that did not happen. What did happen is that each stage I have gone through has, I believe, prepared me for the next one by giving me the learning experience, tools, and strength to continue my journey.

This is a blatantly honest account of my life describing how I not only survived some pretty horrific events, but also the joys, remarkable gifts, and people in my life. Some of these people that I call my angels are my family, true friends, and sometimes even total strangers.

I have come to realize over time that some of my decisions I have made were because I never felt loved or deserving enough to have a good man in my life, and I often mistook some emotions for love. When a problem occurred, I thought I could somehow fix it, or in certain circumstances I found myself in too deep, and I could not get out of a situation. I have always tried to live my life with love, respect, and integrity. I have also tried my best to help people, not for the accolades or that-a-girl, but because it is the right thing to do. It is who I am, and it is what's in my heart.

All I have been able to do is the best I can. I am very much aware of all the mistakes I have made, but I believe the most important thing is that I have learned from them. I know not only how lucky I am to be alive, but also that I did not take the road of self-destruction with drugs, alcohol, or worse.

Throughout my journey, I have learned to love myself, to be angry when I should, to forgive when necessary, and to heal the scattered sections of my life that have now been woven into one. It has allowed me to become a whole person and brought me to where I am today.

If even one experience I have written about can help someone get through a situation similar to what I have shared and to bring them hope or a smile, then I have accomplished what I intended in writing this book.

1

Growing Up

My mom told me when I was born that she named me after two movie stars: Michele Morgan and Michele Lee. Little did I know there would be times some people would actually compare my life to a Hollywood movie.

I came into this world on October 28, 1955, on a cold snowy afternoon in Chicago, Illinois. My mom said the only thing she remembered from that day was the nurse giving her three little pills, and three days later, she woke up to a baby girl. My parents, Alfonso and Carolyn Sandoval, had nine children, and I am number five.

My memories of my early childhood include both good and painful ones. I can remember lying in my bed when I was four years old, and my uncle who was living with us would come into my room and hurt me. I was just a little girl, but I knew something did not feel right. He would wake me up with his foul smelling breath and tell me not to say a word or move. I will never forget those visits that went on until I was six or seven years old. When I would tell my mom about it, she would just get angry with me and tell me to be quiet because her brother would never do such a thing.

You see, my mother was an alcoholic and as far back as I can remember, there were always bottles of whiskey hid around the house. You could look under any couch cushion, in the clothes hamper, or cupboard and there was always a bottle somewhere. Mom would buy her liquor by the half-gallon and then fill her pint and half-pint bottles. As I got a little older, I would pour some of the whiskey out and try to disguise it with tea, but she always knew. There were times my mom would send me up the street to a neighbor's house to go play. The next thing I knew, the police would come and get me, and take me back home. They told me that my mom had reported me as a runaway.

On New Year's Eve while my parents were having a party one year, a boy named Bill who was the son of my mom's friend, was home on leave from the Navy. Bill and I and were sitting in his car out in front of my house. Along with my younger sisters, there were also several adults outside in the front yard as well. My mom started screaming accusations at this boy that he was attacking me. He and I were just talking, and nothing improper was happening. This young man's career could have been ruined and charges could have been brought against him for no reason at all. As a child, sometimes the embarrassment was just too much to take.

Not all my childhood memories are bad; some of my best memories were of spending time at my grandparents or my Auntie Adeline's house. My grandma was small in stature but oh my goodness, you never messed with Grandma. She had the most loving, caring heart in the world. When we would visit my grandparents, my grandma always had homemade tortillas waiting for us or was in the process of making them. There was always great food cooking, and delightful smells filled the air. At my grandparents' house, respect, and love were always first, and you felt it the moment you walked in their door. My Auntie Adeline's house was what I considered a safe haven. We would do things like go to the Teen Fair in Denver or listen to my older cousin and his band practice at her house. While visiting my Aunt, there was always something to do there, and I felt I could just be a kid and feel safe.

I went to Catholic School from the first grade through the eighth grade. There is one memory that I will never forget. In the Catholic Church, first confessions are part of the process for a child who will be receiving First Holy Communion. On the day of my first confession when I was in the second grade, I went into the confessional and said, "Bless me Father, for I have sinned. This is my first confession and my sins are: I stole a car, I robbed a bank, and I said a bunch of swear words at my brothers and sisters. For these and for all my sins I am very very sorry."

SHATTERED PIECES, LOVING HEART

The priest was on the other side of the confessional; all I could hear was what sounded like a muffled laugh and Father clearing his throat. He kept asking me, "Are you sure my child?" I finally broke down in tears and told him that I had not done any of these things but that I thought I was supposed to have sins to confess. Since I had none to tell him, I thought I should make some up. I did have penance to say that day, but I will never forget the patience and kindness that Father showed to me when I was so frightened and obviously confused. The next day in class, of course we all learned the true meaning of confession.

We use to put on 'musical shows' in my backyard for all the neighbors. I have always loved to sing and so everyone would convince me to put a show on. We would hang sheets and blankets on the clotheslines for the curtains. I would stand on a milk crate, and we would invite the entire neighborhood over and charge them a dime to get in. I would sing my little heart out, and then all us kids would go and buy penny candy at the store with all of our riches.

I remember some of our best family times were at the drive-in movies. We would pile in the station wagon; bring sandwiches and popcorn from home and play on the swings while waiting for the movie to start. Another great time was every year when my family would gather around the TV together and watch the *Wizard of Oz*. To this day I am still afraid of that wicked witch. I would try to watch the movie while peeking through my hands as I covered my eyes, hoping that the ugly green woman with her flying monkeys would not come through the screen and grab me. The other kids would tease me relentlessly and try to scare me even more.

Our family vacations were fun most of the time, but on one of our trips to Hoover Dam, I came down with a bad case of the measles. My mom and I stayed at the motel while the others went to the Petrified Forest and Painted Desert. On the drive back home we had to cross the state line, and I was afraid the guards at the border might keep me. I was hiding in the back of the car with a blanket over my head while begging my parents to turn the car back around. I told them the people in Arizona might not want a little girl with red dots all over her body on their side of the state line. Mom and Dad got quite the laugh out of that statement.

My brothers, sisters, and I are quite the group. I have always looked up to and admired my oldest sister Judy; I have been her "Bug in hair" or "Bug" my whole life. I got this name, because she says I used to give her butterfly kisses and move my nose back and forth in her hair from the time I was just a tiny little one. Judy had a rough childhood and went through her own personal hard times, but she always managed to be there for us kids. My sister has always been able to make me laugh. No matter what the situation, she has a way of comforting people, not only with words, but also with her sense of humor, which makes it so much easier to get through the pain.

SHATTERED PIECES, LOVING HEART

My brother Bobby was next in line; he and Judy were from my mom's first marriage. Bobby was in Camarillo State Mental Hospital from the time he was a little boy. When Bobby was little, he fell down a flight of stairs. He was given a diagnosis of encephalitis and had experienced grand mal seizures. I remember that if I happened to answer the phone when Bobby would call home, I would get into trouble for accepting the collect calls. We were not to tell anyone where my brother lived because it was a family secret. The one and only time that Bobby came home to visit, he and I planted a garden in the backyard. His visit was only for a week but I do remember he was a gentle soul with a big heart. When I accidentally told one of our neighbors that he was coming home for his visit I got into big trouble. To me it did not matter, he was just my big brother. Bobby died at the age of 24 years old, and I was 12 at the time. When the call came that he died, I cried for a long time. People kept telling me that I did not even actually know him and that I was over-reacting. My heart was sad, and to this day I have never forgotten him.

My sister Diana is two years older than I am and was a fiercely independent free spirit. We used to have the craziest fights; all of us kids would take sides and gang up on each other, and it was up to my sister to try to keep us all in line. Dee always had a very loving heart and her smile always seemed to make everything all right during the hard times when I was little. I am not sure why Dee left home to go live with our neighbors at an early age, but

GROWING UP

I did not see my sister until many years later.

My sister Juanita is one year older than I am. Nita was always the logical one of all of us kids and I used to call her my conscience. Nita would always make sure that we all behaved. She was loving but stubborn at the same time and was a lot of fun to be around. She has always been a no-nonsense kind of girl, but at the same time, she was sensitive to those around her.

After me, my brother Johnny was next in our group. He and I were inseparable when we were little. Johnny could be such a pain and was a typical little brother, but I adored him. He was always Mom's golden boy, and in her eyes he could do no wrong. When my mom would get drunk, she would tell my little brother and I that we were not our dad's biological kids, but I think this made our relationship even stronger.

My brother Jimmy was such a sweet and loving little boy and always tried to protect us. The size of the person did not matter; my brother would, and still does, step up and let others know that they had better not mess with the people he loves. Both my brothers used to pick on us girls however. They would catch grasshoppers and take a long needle and thread, and make a lasso out of them. When my sisters and I would walk outside, they would throw those nasty bugs around us while the grasshoppers were still trying to jump. I am still petrified of those insects.

Laura has always been my beautiful, ray of sunshine. She was a tiny little girl and had long beautiful hair and the biggest brown eyes. She could be so sweet one minute and a little ball of dynamite the next. I think the saying "dynamite comes in small packages" was because of my sister Laura. Throughout the years, Laura has always seen the best in me and if others would give me a hard time or judge me, she always stood up for me and I am very grateful.

Maria is the baby of the family and was biologically born to my Aunt. Mom and Dad went to the hospital one day and came back with a baby girl. Even though she was not biologically born to our parents, she has always been and will always be my baby sister. She is compassionate and has the biggest heart, and she is one of the strongest women I know.

My dad went to Viet Nam in the late 1960's when I was in the seventh grade. I was 20 minutes late walking home from school one day, and Dad took me downstairs and busted my tail with a 2x4 board. He told me it was a reminder while he was away to toe the line, and it worked. It was not a beating but just to get his point across to me.

While my dad was off fighting for our country and trying to survive in a war zone, he would call home and wait hours in the monsoon rains to get through to us. When he was finally able to get a connection, Mom was usually out somewhere with Jack, her new boyfriend, or was too drunk to come to the phone.

A year passed, and it was time for my Dad to come

home. All of us kids were excited; we made signs and cards and got dressed up to go to the airport, only the homecoming was not what we expected. When Dad stepped off the plane, Mom would not even give him a hug. She just shoved divorce papers in his hand and walked away with us kids. I was speechless and could not quit crying. I cannot even imagine the hurt and pain my dad felt. A few hours after returning from the airport, my dad showed up at Jack's house. My dad had been sober for many years, but on that night, he was drunk. He stood in Jack's driveway and yelled, "Whoever is coming with me let's go, and if any of you kids are going to be staying with you mother then stay! If no one comes with me I will blow my head off right here, right now!" All of us kids had about two minutes to decide who we were going to live with. My older sister Nita and little brother Johnny decided to go with my dad, and I would not see them until many years later. I stayed with my mom, along with my youngest brother and two sisters

I now attribute my dad's behavior that night to *Post Traumatic Stress Disorder* (PTSD), from his time in Viet Nam, as well as the homecoming my mom gave him at the airport. I am sure it must have seemed as if my dad's world shattered all within a few hours.

After Mom and Jack were married, we moved a few times and then eventually settled into a beautiful house in Aurora Hills, Colorado. At first things seemed to be okay, and then Jack started getting ugly with us kids. When I was in the 7th grade, I started my monthly cycle and had stomach cramps. Jack called me upstairs and started hitting me in the stomach with his fists while calling me horrible names and saying that I was pregnant. He told me he did not want someone like me living in his house and giving him a bad reputation. I honestly did not know what sex was or what the names he was calling me meant.

Not long after this happened, my mom was in the hospital to have major surgery for cancer. On the day of her discharge, my friend Debbie came over and we decided to surprise Mom and Jack. We cleaned the house from top to bottom, made banners, blew up balloons, and were having a great time. When Mom and Jack walked in the door, Jack told Debbie to go home and then he started yelling at me for having company over. He took off his dreaded belt once again, and he swung it at me. My mom blocked his belt buckle with her hand, which was going towards my face, and she ended up in the emergency room getting several stiches. Had it not been for my mom blocking the buckle it would have hit my face. *I despised my stepfather as much as a 12-year-old girl was capable of for everything he had done to us.*

One night, I snuck out of the house and walked around the block see my friend Kirk. His mom and my mom were best friends, and Kirk was my first serious crush. We were spending time in his basement, listening to music when one thing led to another. A few hours later I walked home, and when I turned the corner, there was a police car in front of my house. I knew that I was in trouble. When the officer saw I was okay he left, and I went upstairs to talk to my mom.

I had always thought that my mom and I could talk about anything. I started to explain to her that I had lost my virginity to Kirk and then she slapped me. I believed at that moment I probably deserved it, but I was in not prepared for what happened next. My mom called me a liar and a tramp, and slapped me again, only this time harder. I was crying and trying to tell her how sorry I was for disappointing her. She pulled me by the hair, looked at me with the most hateful eyes and said, "It's not because I am disappointed in you, you dumb little tramp, it's because Kirk is mine! I slept with him, and he would never have sex with you; you are a liar, Michele!" How in the heck does one respond to that? Kirk was 15 years old, and my mother had sex with him? It was at that moment that I decided to run away from home at 14 years old and never looked back.

2

You and Me Against the World

I found out I was pregnant with my first child when I was 17 years old. I was shocked, happy and frightened all at the same time. I lived with my friend Dian for the first few months of my pregnancy, and then I rented an apartment.

One night while at Eu-Can Bowling Center, I was watching some friends bowl during their league. I ran into my friend Liza and her husband Jim, both of whom I had known for quite a while. Liza told me that she and Jim had recently been talking, and since they had a spare room in their home, they wanted to invite me to come to stay with them. Liza's husband was a detective for the local police department, and Liza was home alone quite a bit because of her husband's hours. Since I was single and lived alone, they thought Liza and I would be good company for each other and that I would have someone close by with my delivery date coming up. I accepted their kind offer and started to settle into their house.

I had been living at Liza's for about a week, and on the night of April 3rd, I was having a hard time getting comfortable. As the night went on and into the next morning, I was in severe pain in both my back and stomach. When I called my doctor, he said to meet him at the hospital. On the way to the hospital, I got sick in Liza's car. Her car was a 1955 Classic T-Bird, and she called it "her baby." Liza was yelling and cursing at me all the way to the hospital. When we pulled up to the front door she told me to get out of her car and that I needed to make other arrangements, because I would not be going back to her house after I delivered my baby. I had given up my apartment the week before to move in with her, so I had no idea what I was I was going to do.

I waddled into the hospital and checked myself in. I was in so much pain; I was fighting against it and not trying to relax, which made the pain even more intense. My friend Dian had come up to the hospital later that day with a few of our friends to keep me company. I was very thankful Dian showed up, but I still felt very much alone.

After 17 hours of difficult labor and a few complications with my delivery, at 9:18 p.m. on April 4, 1974, I gave birth to my incredible little girl. My heart already knew she was going to be a girl, and I had picked out the name Christina Marie. My daughter weighed in at eight pounds even and was beautiful.

A few hours after my delivery while holding my daughter

in my arms, I was crying with happiness that God had blessed me with this perfect little miracle, and yet I was trying to figure out where I would take her home. I was listening to music playing in my hospital room, and at that moment the song *You and Me Against the World* came on the radio. The words to this song described exactly how I was feeling, and this would become my daughter's and my song.

The second day of my admission, my friend Barbara who was a police officer came to visit me. She had heard what had happened from Liza's husband Jim. Apparently, Liza's husband was angry with his wife for the way she had treated me, and my friend Barbara was furious. Barbara told me that when the hospital discharged me, she wanted my baby and me to come and stay with her. I could not believe she was making such a generous offer. I looked at her in disbelief, and I promised her that I would not overstay my welcome if she really wanted us to come. She told me not to worry about anything and welcomed us into her home. During our stay, my friend was amazing to both my little one and me. Christina and I stayed with my friend for six weeks, and then we moved into our own place.

Thank you, Barbara, I have never forgotten your kindness or your compassionate heart, and to me you are an angel. I find it ironic that the woman who helped Christina and me when my daughter first came into this world – a time when we needed someone's help the most – was in law enforcement, and that all these years later, my daughter chose the same career path.

3

One Last Beer

In 1975, my friend Dian and I were at a party when a man walk up and started talking to us. He told us his name was Jerry, and I was very attracted to him. Jerry and I had a great time that night. We danced, drank a few beers, and enjoyed each other's company.

Jerry and I saw one another every weekend when he would come home from out of town while working for his dad's company. It seemed like the perfect relationship, and after a few months, he moved back to Albuquerque and we moved in together. The times that Jerry and I had together in the beginning of our relationship were great. We would go to his parents' cabin, or we would take the kids to the zoo for example; we were always busy doing something together. He was loving and attentive, and I truly was in love this man.

In due time, I started finding out things were not as

perfect as they seemed to be. Jerry would drink too much, and he and I would get into arguments. The arguments started to turn into name-calling, which eventually escalated into more.

One night while we were at a local bar, it started getting late and I was ready to go home. Jerry wanted to stay and keep drinking. He kept telling me to go ahead and go home, and he would find a ride. I kept asking him if he was sure, and he kept insisting that I go. A few hours later, I was jolted out of my sleep by Jerry grabbing me by the hair and nightshirt. He started hitting me and then knocked me into the bathroom wall, and then he pulled me up again and slammed me up against the bathtub. He was calling me names while screaming at me as to why I had left him at the bar. The more I tried to reason with him the angrier he became. When I knew he was asleep, I snuck out and called my friend Dian, and she, her mom, and sister came to get me.

Jerry's violence was something I had not experienced before. He kept apologizing, and I would tell myself that he was a good man and that he'd just had to much to drink that night, along with all the other excuses I could think of for his behavior.

Several months later, we had just finished eating dinner and were settling down to watch TV when there was a knock at the door. By the time I reached the door a man and woman burst in. The man called Jerry outside, and the woman he was with grabbed me, telling me to get my kids and to go into the bathroom. Stunned and confused, I started to fight with her and then she pulled out a knife. A few minutes later, Jerry came back inside and said "Michele you need to go with this guy." I looked at him in disbelief and kept asking him what he was talking about, he looked at me and yelled "Michele go!" I looked over at the woman with the knife, and she was standing right next to my two little ones. I slowly stood up, walked towards the door and went outside, not knowing what to expect.

When I got down the steps, the man walked up next to me and said, "Just walk with me." I was confused and scared to death, and then he showed me he was carrying a gun. Our mobile home was parked behind a motel, and the man was walking us in that direction. He told me that he made a deal with Jerry, and he and Jerry were going to be trading his wife for me for the night. This man started telling me in detail all things he was going to do to me. I was trying to get a grasp on what was going on while praying to myself. The closer we came to the motel, the more I was shaking, and my heart was beating so fast I thought for sure it was going to jump out of my chest. For some reason, I was able to talk to this man in a calming voice, while trying not show him how truly frightened I was. I told him I knew in my heart that he did not want to hurt me and that my kids needed me. I also told him I was in love with Jerry and that I would not feel right sleeping with someone else. Many other things came pouring out of my mouth it seemed from nowhere. As frightened as I was, I was not begging him, but trying to reason with him somehow.

As quickly as it all started, the man took me by the arm back to my house and did not say another word to me. When we walked in my front door, the man pulled Jerry out of the house and started beating on him. While hitting Jerry, he was yelling at him for not telling me about the deal they had made. There was no way that I could comprehend that Jerry had made the kind of deal these people were saying that he had, and my heart would not let me believe it either.

When Jerry came back inside, the woman left with the man, and he started hitting her out in front of my house. He was yelling at her for not being able to persuade me to be with him. The woman kept yelling that she had done her part, and wanted to know why he had not just done to me what he had planned. He screamed at her that I was more of a lady in the short time when he and I we were walking, then the tramp she had been all the years they had been together. Absolutely, none of this made any sense to me at all. The one thing I did know was that it had to have been some kind of divine intervention the way the words came out of my mouth, and how calm I was on the outside and the fact the man did not touch me.

We had no phone in our mobile home, so for the rest of the night while Jerry lay in the bedroom in severe pain from his beating, I paced the living room floor while peeking out the windows and hoping that those maniacs did not come back.

ONE LAST BEER

Mother's Day was a few days away and I had forgotten Jerry's mom was coming to pick me up to go shopping the next day. When his mom came by the next morning, Jerry stayed, hidden in our bedroom and the kids and I left with his mom. I told his mom some story that Jerry had made up for me to tell her as to why he had not seen her when she stopped by. While we were out, Jerry's mom knew something was very wrong and kept asking me about it. I finally told her the truth about what happened. She was very upset as I expected and then thanked me for telling her. She dropped the kids and I back at home, gave me a big hug, and told me not to worry and that everything would be okay.

Later that night I heard a knock at the door, and I thought I would jump out of my skin. Looking out, I saw it was Jerry's older brother Al, and he asked me to explain to him what had happened the night before. After I told him, he handed me a gun and told me to use it for protection, and he said would be back soon. Jerry's brother came back the next day with his truck and told us were going to move in with him and his wife, and I was very grateful.

After talking to the local police, we found out that the man who broke into our house was from out of state. He had violated his parole and was supposed to be heading back to jail, but instead, he and his wife ended up in Albuquerque.

A few weeks after we had moved, I found out I was pregnant. When I told Jerry, he was unusually quiet and would not even look at me for a few days. While alone one afternoon in the house, Jerry called me a tramp and a liar and told me I was not pregnant. He started hitting me and was telling me that if it were true, he was going to make sure that I was not pregnant for very long. The next day when I woke up, I was in a lot of pain, and started bleeding. I went to the doctor, and he told me I was eight weeks pregnant but that he could not detect a fetal heartbeat. I knew the baby had died, but my heart and my head could not reconcile this.

The doctor told me that I had a spontaneous abortion, which is another name for a miscarriage. He also said that I needed a procedure called a D & C, or *dilation and curettage*, which is a surgical procedure to open the cervix and remove whatever tissue remains in the uterus. I am Catholic, and because of my religious beliefs, when the doctor told me I had had a spontaneous abortion, my heart sank. Abortion to me is a mortal sin. Just being in the room and knowing that they were taking my child out of me during the procedure was more than I could take. The worst part was that when I looked over at the jar, I could see little parts of my baby, and I knew I would never be the same.

Years later I found peace, finally understanding that I had not committed murder and that the baby had already-been gone. Because they had used the word abortion, it took my priest to persuade me that I should not carry the guilt which had lain so heavy on my heart. After this happened I left Jerry, and he went to his parents' house to stay for a while.

Several months after I left Jerry he came over to my house one night, and he looked terrific. He said he was doing well and he genuinely seemed to have changed his life. I knew he had been living at his parents' house and I honestly believed he was a changed man. On Jan 21st, which happened to fall on Jerry's birthday, I conceived what was to be my last child.

Even though we were not together any longer, this time Jerry's reaction was very different from my previous pregnancy. He was telling everyone he was going to be a dad and that he was making plans for the baby's arrival. I told Jerry that I was going to raise this child, and if he wanted to be a part of his baby's life, it would be on my terms.

On the morning of October 14th, I woke up with severe back pain, only this time it was much different than I had experienced before. I arrived at the hospital and after my doctor examined me, he said I was in labor but not progressing as I should. He started an IV of Pitocin to increase my contractions, and then he broke my water to try to help my labor along. The doctor said he knew I should not be having so much pain because I was not dilating at all. He ordered an x-ray and told me that I had a large kidney stone which I needed to pass before I could deliver the baby. The nurses kept a close watch on me, and after a while, the doctor came in and said "Michele, if you do not deliver this baby by 6:30 p.m. I am going to have to perform a cesarean section."

After 30 hours of hard labor, I was finally able to pass the kidney stone. Jerry finally showed up as they were taking me to the delivery room. The nurses were not happy, and they could not understand why he only showed up at the last minute and not when I needed him most. When asked, Jerry just casually said he was busy. At 6:20 p.m. on October 15, 1977 my beautiful seven pound one ounce daughter, Shawna Renee decided to make her entrance into this world. She was going to come out when she was ready, and that was all there was too it. If she had waited another ten minutes, the doctor would have performed the C-Section. I was so happy and felt very blessed. My mom and Jerry's mom came into the recovery room to see me, I was actually surprised because I do not remember them even being at the hospital, but was extremely happy to see them both.

Jerry and I would try to remain friends for the sake of our daughter, but as far as I was concerned, that was as far as I would ever let it go again. My brother Johnny called one afternoon and told me Jerry was staying in a motel and wanted to discuss something with him. My brother told me Jerry was on a drinking binge and that he had a gun. He said that Jerry would yell horrible accusations about me in one breath and then tell my brother, while crying, how he missed me the next. Jerry also told Johnny he was going to kill me and then kill himself. Johnny had called to warn me, and then I called some family members, but I do not think many people believed me at that point.

Shortly after this incident, Jerry went into a long-term treatment facility. He made it through the program, and he seemed to be doing remarkably well until a year later.

A few weeks after the kids and I had moved to Socorro, New Mexico, I received a phone call from my sister Maria who told me that Jerry had died. Jerry and one of his friends had decided to go target practicing after an all-night drinking binge. They were out behind the Albuquerque Airport and Jerry's van had run out of gas. His friend had walked to the nearest gas station to find some gas and while he was gone, Jerry had written a note, picked up a gun, and shot himself in the head.

Jerry clung to life for another 12 hours. During this time, his parents tried to get word to me, but I never received the messages. Jerry's mom told me he might have been waiting to die so he and I could say our final good-bye. In the suicide note Jerry left, he stated that he could no longer handle being sober, yet he did not want to live his life with alcohol any longer and was ashamed about it. Jerry asked that all of his belongings go to our beautiful daughter Shawna, then he sent his love and asked for his parents and God's forgiveness, and finally fired the gun.

On September 10, 1982, at age 26, Jarrod Laurant Wright was dead. After a full investigation, the police ruled his death as a self-inflicted gunshot wound to the head. The morning of the shooting, my former neighbors at the apartment complex that I had just moved out of told me that Jerry had suddenly showed up there. He was pounding on my old apartment door as well as the neighbors' doors, yelling something about wanting to find Shawna and me. I am not sure of what might have happened if my kids and I had still been living in our old apartment on that day, but I am very thankful we were not. After his death, several people told me how sorry they were that they did not believe me about his physical abuse and the depths of what we had gone through.

Do I wish things had been different at times throughout the seven years Jerry and I knew each other? I am sure you know the answer to this: of course I do. Do I have any regrets being with this man? No, because whatever journey I had to take, the Lord blessed me with my beautiful daughter, and I would not change one second to have her in my life.

4

I Thought I Knew You

My daughter Tina and I were walking outside Eastdale Shopping Center in Albuquerque on April 4, 1981. It was Tina's seventh birthday and we out shopping for her. We were having a terrific time when I heard a male voice saying "Mikki is that you?" I turned around and saw it was Craig. Craig was someone I had known since the 7th grade. We talked for a few minutes, and he asked me for my phone number. I did not see a problem with it since I had known him for so long. I gave him my phone number, and Tina and I went on with our day.

Craig called me that night, and we talked for hours. He was living in Socorro, which was an hour's drive from Albuquerque. We spent a lot of time on the phone, and every weekend when he came home, we would spend all our time together. It was beginning to feel as though we were a family. Eventually Craig asked me to marry him, and I accepted his proposal. We had a little ceremony up in the Sandia Mountains, stood before a judge, and became husband and wife.

Shortly after Craig and I were married, there were signs of trouble. The first thing that caught my attention after moving to Socorro was that my husband did not want a phone in the house. My neighbors were kind enough to let me use their phone for messages, in case my family back in Albuquerque needed to reach me.

One day, my neighbor's son came over and told me that I had a call from home. The call was from my sister Maria, and she told me that Shawna's dad, Jerry, had died. After talking with my sister, I called my brother and told him I wanted to come home for the funeral and to please come and get the kids and me.

When I walked back in my house, I was crying. Craig looked at me and yelled, "What is wrong with you, and why are you sniveling?" I did not say anything and then a few minutes later he yelled at me again, "What is your problem Mikki?" I mumbled something about Jerry dying, and Craig backhanded me. He screamed, "Why are you crying for him?" Then he started slapping and punching me, telling me to shut up and quit crying. He threw me on the bed and kept hitting me with one hand while he had his other hand around my throat. At that moment, my brother arrived. Johnny told Craig he was taking the kids and me back to Albuquerque with him.

Once I was back in Albuquerque, I knew I did not

want to go back to Craig. Jerry's parents asked me if the kids could stay with them for a few weeks and I agreed. With everything that had just happened with my husband, and Jerry's death a few days before, I felt I needed a little time to regroup. Jerry's parents were remarkable, and loving people and I think they needed to be around my little ones as much as my little ones needed their grandparents. I rented an apartment and the kids and I started settling in.

A few months later Craig contacted me and he told me he had moved to Wyoming. He kept telling me he was sorry, he was going to counseling for his temper, and it would never happen again. He was living in a small town, had a great job as an oil rigger, and rented a nice house for us. After months of him trying to convince me and knowing I had taken marriage with him, I eventually gave in, and the kids and I moved to Wyoming.

The kids and I had only been in Wyoming for a few weeks and one evening the doorbell rang. Standing at the door was a woman who looked to be about 5 months pregnant. Craig did not invite her in but he walked outside and talked to her. When I approached Craig later that night about the woman who came to the house, he told me since I was not able to give him kids; he went out and found someone who could. Craig started hitting me for asking him questions and getting into his business, and I knew the kids and I were in deep trouble.

I could not just leave Craig not only because of my

financial situation, but he had quit his job a few days after the kids and I had moved there. He also told me if I tried to leave him he knew where my sisters, mom, and the rest of the family lived, and he swore to me I would regret it. I was never allowed to go anywhere without Craig I actually felt like a prisoner in my own home.

Christmas was coming up, and Craig went around the corner to get a tree. While he was out, the kids started making the sweetest homemade decorations to surprise him. When he walked in the door, he saw the ornaments and yelled, "What is this crap?" He tore every one of them up and stomped on them. My poor babies were so heartbroken that it devastated my heart.

One night my husband was drunk and he brutally beat and raped me with my little ones there. When he was finished, he got up, walked into the kitchen, and grabbed another beer. Tina walked over to him sat on his lap, and said, "Daddy I love you," she had never called him that in her life. Tina would always call him Craig, but at that moment, he calmed down, went into the bedroom, and passed out cold.

I made sure he was still asleep, and I opened his wallet that was on the dresser, shaking and praying the whole time, I saw there were three $20.00 bills, so I took them. I went back into the living room, and I told the kids to quietly, help me gather some clothes; we put them in a laundry basket and into bags. If Craig woke up, I was going to tell him we were going to do laundry.

My three little ones and I walked for what seemed like

miles in the snow. I am sure it was not that far, but in December walking down the streets in Wyoming while pulling a wagon full of clothes with my three little ones, it sure felt like it. We found a motel and I managed to get a room for us. I asked the clerk if anyone called or looked for us, not to give out any information and please call the police.

A few hours later Craig had found us. The night clerk who had just come on duty happened to know my husband and when the shift changed, the day shift clerk did not tell him of my situation. Craig was pounding on the door and I called the police. When the police arrived they told him to leave or they would take him to jail, but they would not do anything about what had happened at the house earlier. Before Craig found us at the motel, I had called my uncle in Denver, and he was kind enough to wire us bus fare to get home. The next morning I had the police escort us to pick up the money, get a few things from the house, and then escort us to the bus station.

The kids and I settled back in Albuquerque and Craig showed up at my door a few months later thanks to some people we both knew. These people, had seen me around town, followed me home, and then told Craig where the kids and I were living. My husband threatened me once again, telling me every detail of what he would do to me if I did not go with him. I knew him well enough by this time to know that hewould follow through on his threats.

Craig had moved to another small town outside

SHATTERED PIECES, LOVING HEART

of Albuquerque where his parents lived. Out of fear, the kids and I moved there. I thought that if his parents were close by, we might be safe for a short time at least.

About a week later, I was in taking a bath and Craig answered a knock at the front door. The New Mexico State Police were standing at the door and told Craig I needed to call home to Albuquerque immediately. Craig threw open the bathroom door, and yelled, "Now what has your lowlife family done?" I knew something must have been terribly wrong for my sister to get word to me in such a manner.

We went to my in-laws house to use their telephone; I called my sister and she told me our Mom had died. I was in shock and fainted. The next thing I remember was that Craig's parents were following us in their car and that we were driving to Albuquerque. I thought they were being compassionate and helpful because my mom had just died, but within a few hours I would know the real reason.

When we arrived at my sister's house, my mother-in-law told me that Craig was going to stay with me in Albuquerque and that my kids were going back with her and her husband to their house. I started arguing with them because I wanted my kids with me. Craig took me aside and put his knife on my back and then he whispered in my ear "They will be fine they are going with my mom and dad do you understand?" I felt I had no choice and the kids went back with my in-laws.

The next morning was my mom's funeral and when Craig woke up, he looked at me and adamantly said, "I am not going to the service and neither are you Mikki!" I kept asking him what he was talking about and he told me, "You will do as I say if you ever want to see your kids again!" I questioned him why we had driven all the way to Albuquerque just for him to break my heart once again. His reply was, "Because your family would have stuck their nose in our business like they always do had I not brought your sorry self here. My parents took your kids back with them so you would not run your mouth to your family about our business or try to leave me." I told my family I was just too upset over our mom's death, and could not walk in the church. I was devastated beyond words of course, but my priority was to get back to my kids and make sure that they were okay, and I was not going to take any chances. Craig and I went home that same day and picked up the kids. I kept praying to myself repeatedly, "Please Lord, help me to figure out a way to get my kids and myself out safe, once and for all."

The next day, I was in the back yard hanging the laundry. Across the fence from our house, I saw a woman outside and she waved to me, I did not dare say hi but I waved back to her. I did not realize how important this woman was about to become in my life.

Over the course of the next two days after getting back from Albuquerque, Craig would be sitting in the rocking chair, with his loaded shotgun rocking back and forth while asking me, "You'd never leave me would you Mikki?" He did this several times and then on the morning of the third day, he pointed his shotgun right in my face and said, "You'd never leave me would you Mikki?" I could not take it anymore, I was down to 89 pounds with my weight, and I was a nervous wreck and physically and emotionally spent. I had to take my chances and get my kids out of there for the last time. All I kept thinking about is the way my mom had just died a few days before, and we had to get away!

After we finished lunch that day, I concocted some story that I had to go to the WIC (Women's, Infants, and Children) office. WIC is a food and nutrition program that helps both pregnant women and families with young children; it provides education, food, and support. I told Craig that I had completely forgotten about the appointment with everything that had been going on with my mom. Craig wanted Shawna to stay at the house with him, but I told him I would not get WIC unless she was with me in person. I also told Craig we would take the bus. That way he would not have to wait for us while we were at the appointment, because it would probably take quite a while. After spending a few hours of trying to convince him to let me go, he finally screamed to go ahead, and then added, "You better be back real soon, don't make me come looking for you Mikki!" This was the first time he had let me out of his sight and I knew I finally had my one and only chance.

I THOUGHT I KNEW YOU

I saw Craig watching as Shawna and I walked around the corner. I held on to my little girls hand and prayed. Shawna and I walked around the block out of his view, and we ran up to the woman's house that I had seen in the backyard a few days before. I knocked on her door, and she invited me in. She told me her name was Mary, and I explained my situation to her. I also told her that I was very worried because Tina and Jeremy would be out of school at any time and walking home from their bus stop. Mary told me her son was in middle school but would be home soon, and she would have him meet my kids at their bus stop and bring them to me. Within a few minutes, her son walked in the door.

My kids and I always had a code word so that if someone tried to pick them up without telling them a certain word, the kids knew not to go with them. I told Mary's son the code word, and I held my breath waiting for him to get back with Tina and Jeremy. Within a few minutes, they all walked up confused, but safe and sound. Craig had missed seeing the kids by minutes; my neighbor could see him walking around the neighborhood knocking on doors. We got into Mary's car, which was in the garage, and the kids and I hid down on the floorboards. I asked her to take me to a pawnshop, I had no money, but I did have my wedding set. I pawned my rings, which gave me enough money to get a motel room on the far side of town where Mary dropped us off.

Once inside the motel room, I tried calling back home

to Albuquerque several times to reach someone and I was finally able to talk to my friend Bob Miller. Bob had always been like a big brother to me since I was a young girl, he told me to sit tight, not to answer the motel room door for anyone, and he was on his way.

The town we lived in was a 4-hour drive from Albuquerque and true to his word four hours later, Bob and his friend Terry arrived. I was so relieved and grateful. While Terry stayed with the kids, Bob took me to get some of the kids and my clothes out of my house. Bob was a big man, but Craig was no small person either. However, I knew I was safe with Bob.

When we got to my house and started walking up towards the door Craig opened it up. Bob was standing to the side of me, and Craig kept saying I needed to come in the house but no way that was going to happen. Bob saw that Craig had a knife in his hand, and his shotgun leaning up against the wall. Craig lunged towards me to try to drag me inside the house, Bob shoved me out of the way and yelled at me to get in the car, and we headed back to the motel to get the kids. While leaving town, Bob saw Craig and another man driving around in a truck with shotguns. The kids hid until we out of the city limits.

I found out after my kids and I had moved near his parents that Craig's father worked for the local law enforcement agency. You would think Craig's parents would have been right there to help me and my kids. However, that did not happen; in fact, it was quite the opposite.

When I returned to Albuquerque, I was granted an order of protection against Craig.

Some of my friends offered to drive me back to my house to help me get the kids and my stuff with their truck. I called ahead and talked to the state police not the local authorities, and let them know I was coming into town. I brought my paperwork and the state police escorted me to the house, and when we arrived, Craig was not there.

The first thing I saw when I was walking up the sidewalk, was a pile of clothes, papers, baby books, baby jewelry, pictures of my mom, and even the rosary my dad had given to me. Everything was in a pile of ashes. I looked at my belongings with tears in my eyes, felt angry for a minute, and then realized of course what really mattered, was we were all okay.

I stopped over at Mary's, the woman who had been so kind to my kids and me the day we left. I brought her a bouquet of flowers and I wanted to let her know we were all right, and how truly grateful I was for her kindness. I told her she was indeed an angel here on earth, and she probably saved our lives. She was very happy to see me, and told me she often wondered how we were doing.

It took me awhile to find Craig to serve him with divorce papers, he was living in California, but my attorney was able to track him down. The judge ordered in my final divorce decree that Craig is never to have any contact with my family or me again. Craig and I were legally married for three years and only physically together for eight of the most horrific months of mine, and my children's life.

I have never been able to forgive him to this day. For him to hurt me was one thing, but what my kids had to witness is completely another. I am grateful that Jeremy and Shawna have no memory of the time we were with Craig, but Tina remembers every detail and that is bad enough. Most important, I am grateful that he never tried to touched any of the kids.

I just recently found out through public court records, that I am not the only one of Craig's wives that my former husband had abused. When I read this, I felt so sad for the other women that were also his victims. I know there are countless women, who are in abusive relationships and have to endure their own private hell on a daily basis. When I read that I was not the only one Craig had victimized, it made quite an impact on me.

I have learned that an abuser will alienate you from your friends and family, so they can have complete control over you. They sometimes will threaten your loved ones who are far away and this is one reason I believe Craig kept moving us. When a woman is battered, it can be extremely difficult to get away from the situation. People ask why you cannot just leave. There can be several different reasons why a woman cannot or will not leave the situation. She may fear for her life, or the life of her family. She may not have the resources to leave in order to survive.

There can be many other factors as well; her self-esteem could be so low she does not think she deserves any better. Sometimes when a person only hears negative things from people from the time they are young, they start to believe this and think this is all they deserve. In addition, for some woman a pattern develops, she sometimes does not know how to break free of the cycle of being in abusive relationships. I urge any person who is going through physical, emotional, or mental abuse to seek help immediately. Unlike twenty-seven years ago, there are now wonderful programs and resources available to help people who are victims of abuse.

5

I Am Home Michele

Growing up with my mom is what I would describe as emotionally chaotic. There was always a sense of unpredictability that never went away. It took me until five years ago to learn how to be angry with my mom, to forgive her, and then finally to heal from the all the hurt and pain.

My mom was born in 1924; she was the oldest of four kids. I do not know much about my mom's early life except for what she wanted to share with me. What I do know is her mother died of cancer when she was a very young girl. She told me her father-committed suicide, when she was around 17 years old, because he fell in love her and could not live with the shame. My mom told me of at least three times where she had been raped at a very young age. I think because of the pain and anguish throughout her life, my mom fell into a bottle, and never found her way out. Because of my mom's disease I used to think I could deal with the hurt and pain she caused and I would make excuses for her behavior.

Alcoholism is not only the person's illness who is drinking, but those who are close to them, as well. When my mom was sober, she was a loving, giving, and caring woman. My mom was a woman, who was so insecure, and her confidence was so low, it would break my heart. It seemed to me at times she did not know right from wrong but I always loved her and I believe I knew what was in her heart. No matter what we had gone through, she was still my mom. She would always tell me she knew without a doubt that I loved her, I was her girl, and I would always try to be there for her.

When I received the news my mom had died, it devastated me. No one deserves to have gone through what she had to endure and to have their life taken in such a horrific way. At the age of 59 years old, my mom had been beaten to death beyond recognition. None of us kids could even say our final goodbye to her.

The last time I saw my mom alive, she and her boyfriend Howard drove me to the bus station. Mom was drunk and she and I had a big fight that night. When I think back now, I think she was afraid to stay at her boyfriend's house, but she would not tell me this; instead, she expressed her fear as anger and took it out on me. Mom and I spoke on the phone twice again within a two-week period after I left. During our conversations, she told me she knew I loved her, we both apologized for the fight we had, then she said,

"Moms and daughters fight sweetheart, don't worry about it." For many years, I had to live with the guilt and myself, knowing that she and I were fighting the last time I saw her. I always questioned myself, why I didn't just put up with her drunkenness on that day and keep my mouth shut.

I had received a letter from my mom saying she was afraid for her life. Her boyfriend Howard and his friend Clifford wanted my mom to prostitute herself, and she had refused. I tried many time to reach her but was unsuccessful. Three days after the last letter arrived, I received word my mom had died. I gave the letters my mom had sent to me over to the police department after her death.

There was an autopsy performed which showed her cause of death was a *cerebral hematoma caused by blunt-force trauma to the head*. The most confusing part to me is that the police did not do anything about it. I never understood how an autopsy report could state that homicide had not been ruled out and yet, nothing was ever done it seemed to further the investigation. In my opinion, I think the authorities chose to ignore my mom's death. It seemed to me since everyone knew she was an alcoholic, they could have cared less.

A short time after mom died, my brother and I went to the apartment where she had been living, to see if any of her belongings were there. The two men my mom had written me about Clifford and Howard were in the living room and were making rude remarks such as, "Hey, Michele, it sure does smell like someone just died huh?"

And then one of them asked me, "How does it feel to know your mom died right in this room and in that very spot?" These men were saying unthinkable, horrible things like that. My brother told me to go outside and wait for him. I do not know what he said to them but my little brother did not want me anywhere those men who were speaking to me like that. The only belongings of Mom's we found at the apartment was a small wooden plaque that I gave her when I was a little girl, which she had saved all those years and a set of electric rollers my little sister had given to her.

I had run into both Clifford and Howard a short time after my mom died. My first encounter was while I was bartending at the Veterans Hall. I went into work one day and saw Howard sitting at the bar. I turned around and immediately froze in my tracks but did not say a word to him. He recognized me and started yelling at me about how he did not kill my mom and that I had to believe him. My manager was sitting at the bar, so I walked over and stood by him, thinking that he would tell this horrible person to be quiet or leave. He did not say a word and just continued drinking his beer. I handed him my keys, clocked out, and quit my job.

And Clifford, I ran into while attending a private college. I found out by chance he was a financial-aid advisor they had recently hired when I went into the administration office. I needed to see an advisor and when I walked by the new hires desk, I saw Clifford's nameplate which

I AM HOME MICHELE

I recognized right away I looked up and it was him. He recognized me and gave me a look as if to say, do not say a word. I was extremely upset when I saw him, so I walked out of the school and never went back. A few days later, I called the administrator of the college to explain why I was withdrawing. I asked her if she knew the kind of people she had hired to work with students, and what kind of background checks, if any, were required of their employees. The administrator told me that Clifford had been terminated because he was under investigation for crimes that had been committed on campus.

Mom's former boyfriend Howard died of a heart attack within the year of her death. His son called me one day to tell me this. Apparently, Howard's son had found my mom's address book and was letting people know of his dad's death. Clifford's name came across my desk on a medical bill while I was at work one day. My supervisor called me into her office and asked me what was wrong. She said that I looked pale and was shaking uncontrollably, and she wanted to make sure I was okay. I explained the situation to her, and she looked his record up in the computer. She then told me, "Michele, with what is going on with his health condition, he will not be around much longer if that gives you any peace at all." That was all she said; I left it at that and never mentioned it again.

For eight months after my mom's death, I had horrible terror dreams about how she had died. I could see her face in my dreams crying and screaming for help. I fell asleep one day, I think it was from sheer exhaustion since I had not been sleeping at all. I had a dream that seemed so real to me. In my dream, I walked into my kitchen carrying a bag of groceries in each arm. My mom was standing at my sink doing my dishes. I dropped the groceries while crying and screamed, "Mom, is that you? You are here! You are really here!" In my dream, she walked over and gave me an enormous hug and I could truly feel it. She had her favorite perfume on and I could smell the scent, and when she gave me a kiss on the cheek, I felt it. She held me tight, and she said to me, "Michele, I am home honey, I am home!" At that moment, I woke up, and called everyone I knew to tell them I had talked to my mom. Well of course, they all thought I had totally lost my mind by then and I had to clarify I was sleeping when it happened.

On that day, eight months after my mom had died, my heart truly believes that she had finally found the peace she had never known in life. I also believe my mom was in heaven and wanted me somehow to know that. To this day, 26 years later, I have never again had a night terror or bad dream whatsoever about the way my mom died.

6

Pretend Twins

My little brother Johnny and I were born two years and 12 hours apart. We use to tease people and tell them we were twins, in reality we knew we were not but in our hearts, we always were. My brother was born on October 29th and my birthday is the 28th, so every year for our birthdays there would be a cake with cowboys on one side and ballerinas on the other. One year when Johnny turned five, and I was turning seven, we decided we were going to have a party because Mom and Dad said we could not have one that year. Johnny and I made the invitations, took them to school, and handed them out the next day. My parents knew nothing about this party until one of our classmates parents called to get directions to the house. Mom and Dad had to rush out to buy a cake, toys, and games and we had our party. Johnny and I received a few extra birthday swats that year, but we both agreed it was worth it.

SHATTERED PIECES, LOVING HEART

I always knew there was something special about my little brother, not only because he was extremely intelligent, but mostly because he was such a sensitive person even as a little boy. As he got older, he never lost that sensitivity, which people often mistook for weakness. Johnny and I were separated for years after my parent's divorce, and when we finally found one another again, it was as if we were trying to make up for all our lost time.

While Johnny was living in a small town with our dad as a young boy, he encountered a horrible experience. I believe because of that experience as well as other things that happened in his youth, it left a mark on his soul, heart, and being. One weekend while he was alone some men escaped from the state penitentiary, the men broke into my dad's house, and kept my little brother captive. After Johnny and I were reunited, we talked about his experience for hours at length. I promised him, I would never tell anyone the details of what he shared with me but what I will say, is what he told me on that day is inconceivable, horrible, and into the bowels of hell. After what my brother went through and survived, he was never quite the same again.

Johnny came to stay with me a few times throughout the years. One night, he and I decided to go out to the bar and have a drink, and I found out he was still my protective little brother as he always had been. A man came up to the table and asked me to dance. He was a big man, I knew he worked at the bar, and his name was Kegger. He got this nickname because he could carry a keg of beer on his shoulder with one arm. While on the dance floor, Kegger started getting a little too fresh with me. When Johnny saw this, he headed straight towards us and said to Kegger, "Excuse me, that's my sister you are giving a hard time to. Please take your hands off her!" Kegger asked my brother what he was going to do about it. Johnny pulled his arm back as if to try to hit him. Kegger grabbed my brother's arm, held it for a second, and then he apologized. He told Johnny, "Anyone who is willing to go up against someone my size to defend his sister's honor, is okay in my book!" They shook hands and then Kegger went to the bar and bought us a beer.

Another time, my friend Maxine had been staying at my apartment for a while. Maxine was going out with two men at the same time only one of them did not know this. One of the men she was seeing was a cross-county truck driver, and the other was a member of an outlaw motorcycle gang. The trucker came into town and wanted Maxine, and I to go with him on a quick trip to Arizona. The kids were visiting family, so I agreed to go with Maxine for the weekend.

While we were gone, Maxine's biker boyfriend showed up at my apartment along with some of his friends. Johnny was watching my apartment while I was gone on this trip, and the men that were looking for Maxine kept banging on the door until my brother finally answered it. The men wanted to know where Maxine was. Johnny kept telling them he had no idea where, or even who, she was. These men were demanding, threatening, and intimidating him. The men said they knew that Maxine and I were together, and kept asking Johnny where I was. He of course knew, but there was no way he was going to tell them anything.

My brother was a writer, and they saw his work spread out on the table. When my brother would not answer them, each time they asked him where Maxine and I were, they broke one of his fingers. After six of my brothers fingers were broken, they finally decided he knew nothing and left.

Later that night, when I called to check in, my brother told me what had happened. He also said, it probably was a good idea for me to stay away from my apartment for a few days. I lit into Maxine, and asked her what was going on and how in the world did she get my family and me into the middle of this. I told her what had happened to my little brother. She looked at me and said "I wanted to have a good time, and party with my other man and what happened to your brother is not my problem, stuff happens." I told her I wanted her out of my place that night and had her friend drop me off at my car.

When I saw my brother a few days later, I begged him never do anything like that again, and I told him he should of just let them know where I was. He looked at me with his big hazel, little-brother eyes, gave me a hug, and said, "Sis, I would take a bullet for you and never blink an eye!"

PRETEND TWINS

I am not sure what year it was but Johnny remarried and he and his wife had three children, John, James, and a little girl Ariel. These three little ones were so beautiful, and I fell in love with them. I only had contact with them for the first few years of their lives, but certainly not for like of trying on my part.

Eventually my brother and his wife divorced. Not too long after his divorce, Johnny started having serious, emotional problems and he attempted suicide several times. During one of his attempts, Johnny and another man had made a suicide pact. They drank some kind of poison, leaned up against a tombstone at one of cemeteries and waited to die. My brother was in critical condition and had been put on a respirator. I was so afraid that he would not live. I was able to visit him in the Intensive Care Unit for a few minutes every couple of hours. I tried to hold back my tears, held his hand while praying and begged my little brother to fight for his life. He did pull through, but his condition remained serious for quite a while.

While Johnny was an inpatient in the psychiatric unit at another hospital, some people beat him up pretty bad. He claimed it was the staff and a few patients who attacked him. During this time, some of the doctors at the facility wanted to commit him to the state mental hospital. There was no way; we were going to allow that to happen. We contacted patient advocacy, and they were wonderful and helped us find out what actually happened to him. After a competency hearing, the hospital discharged my brother, and we were able to find Johnny a new doctor. This new doctor was wonderful as well as compassionate, and he seemed to help my brother.

I think the medications Johnny was taking along with the horrific things he had endured his entire life was the cause of his clinical depression. One of the medications my brother was taking has now been associated with people attempting suicide, and many have been successful while on this certain drug.

At one time, my brother Johnny had a false positive test for the *Human Immunodeficiency Virus* (HIV). All this took place in the 1980s. Ignorance and fear, as well as the social stigma attached, was still in the forefront for HIV patients. His doctor waited awhile, and Johnny retook two additional tests at separate intervals, and they were both negative. I of course told my little brother the test was wrong when the first false positive came about but no matter what it showed, I would never leave his side. Some people were ignorant and ostracizing him during this time. People's reactions and attitudes to this made me not only angry, but also very sad.

A few months later Mark and I were getting ready for our wedding day. We only had a few weeks left to go, but unfortunately, things were about to be put on hold. On March 23, 1989, my sister Maria came over to our house. I told my sister her how great it was that she drove over to see our new place. When Maria walked in the house, she told me we should probably sit down, and then said that our brother had died, and his body had been found in the Jemez Mountains.

I think she had to tell me twice because I was not understanding, what she was trying to say. I do not remember, too much else other than telling her, "Okay, I will be right back." I ran out the front door to my neighbors across the street and called Mark, he later told me the only thing I said on the phone to him was "My brother is gone" and I hung up. Mark worked on the other side of town but as soon as I hung up the phone, it seemed like he was home. He said he knew by the sound of my voice he had to get to me as soon as possible.

The Wright's showed up a little while later to pick up my kids to spend a couple of nights at their house. I am not sure who called the kids Grandparents, but I was grateful they did. I did not want my kids to see me in the condition I was in, or for them to have to deal with all the confusion.

After everyone left, I walked outside, sat on the curb and ended up just staring out into the street for a while. I remember going back into the house walking around feeling very alone and cold, no matter how many coats, blankets, or sweaters I had around me I just could not get warm.

People started stopping by as they heard the news of my brother's death. Mark's friends wanted to know how Johnny died, where he died and many other details, but I did not want to talk about it. What I did want was for them to stop asking me their stupid questions. All I knew was that my little brother was gone. Several people were standing around, drinking beer and having a great time it seemed. All I could hear was laughter coming from my kitchen. My brother had just died, and I felt as though they were having a party. I wanted to scream at the top of my lungs to everyone and anyone who could hear me, "Don't you know Johnny just died, my little brother is gone!" I realize now that when we lose someone close to us, sometimes our world as we know it stops, while the rest of the world moves on.

I called my friend Melinda and told her what had happened. She said that she would be over as soon as she got off work. I knew that it would be at least a few hours longer. However, within no time at all, she walked in my house and said, "I locked up the store, and called my boss, now what can I do?" I was so grateful she came over. I remember my friend just holding me while I completely fell to pieces. I managed somehow to get through that day and the next few days.

We made the funeral arrangements and we held my brother's service at Sangre De Cristo Catholic Church. The morning of his service, I was shaking so bad and wandering around aimlessly. Melinda stopped by the house just in case I needed anything and I can certainly say I did. I could not even dress myself that day.

Mark's dad and brother were waiting for us when we arrived at the church. They had never even actually known Johnny other than talking to him once or twice, but it truly touched my heart that they were there. Tina was eight months pregnant, and she had a very difficult time walking through the front door of the church. She was extremely close to her Uncle Johnny. Mark's brother was able to get Tina through the doors. I told my daughter it was okay if she was not able to attend the service, but eventually she did manage to make it inside.

I walked into the church holding Marks hand and his dad walked up and grabbed my other hand, and I did not let go of either one of them throughout the service. I will never forget the compassion that Mark and his family showed my family at that time.

After the funeral, everyone was outside ready to leave. I walked outside for a minute, and then wanted to go back into the church by myself to say one last prayer for my little brother. I walked up to the altar, fell to my knees, and the next thing I remember was people telling me that Mark and his brother had followed me into the church to make sure I was okay, and caught me as I fell back. Apparently, everything had finally caught up with me I just could not handle anymore.

Johnny had been staying with me until shortly before he died. We kept in constant touch and things were going really well for him. He had rented a cabin up in the Jemez Mountains and was writing a book. He had a new girl-friend and was off all his medications except for one. The last time we spoke, my little brother told me he was happy, healthy and was very optimistic about his life.

When they discovered Johnny's body, he did not have

his shirt on, and one boot and his belt was missing as well. My brother's girlfriend had gone back to the Albuquerque area with another man, and she had not reported my brother missing for a few days.

After the funeral, Mark, my brother Jim, and Shawna all went to the Jemez Mountains, which was about an hour from my house. When they returned home they told me that the locals in the area were not very friendly, things were quite suspicious, and out of sorts and most of Johnny's writings were missing.

The medical examiner performed an autopsy and the report stated my little brother died of hypothermia; there was no alcohol and no drugs in his system found other than his prescription medication. The report also stated, Johnny had many bruises all over his body, pine needles in his nose and esophagus, and other suspicious findings.

At the age of 31, John Raymond Sandoval my amazing, beloved, sensitive, loving, funny, and pretend twin little brother was gone. I love you Johnny, I miss you more than words can say and when you left us, a part of me went with you.

Johnny's kids and I just recently reconnected and my heart is overjoyed. My nephew James served eight-years in the Navy and one of his duty stations was over in Spain for several years, he also served in the Gulf War. James is now attending college full time back east. My other nephew John was in the Army and served in the war as well, he is happily married with a wonderful little boy, and has plans to attend college in the spring. My niece Ariel is attending college to become a pharmacology technician and is doing very well. I know their dad is so proud of each one of them.

7

Can I Borrow Your Vacuum?

I moved into an apartment in 1979 with my three little ones Tina was five, Jeremy was four, and Shawna was two years of age. The complex had four apartments on each side of a grassed in yard. Across the courtyard from me one day, I saw a woman standing outside. She was pretty, had long blond hair, and was screaming at the top of her lungs. A few days later, the belt on my vacuum broke. When I saw the blond woman outside again, I asked her if she had a vacuum that I could borrow. She said that she did and then told me her name was Pam. She loaned me her vacuum, and we started talking. This conversation would be the start of a 20-year friendship between us.

Pam was there when Tina started kindergarten. After Pam and I walked Tina to school for her first day of class, she was trying not to laugh too hard at me while I was crying like a baby. Pam and I were always there for each other. When I had pneumonia and was admitted to the hospital in serious condition, Pam only left my side once until my condition stabilized. When Pam was going through a very difficult time in her life, her three kids came to stay with me for several months. Her kids, along with my three kids stayed in my tiny apartment. It was crowded, but I was all they had during that time, and there was no way I was about to let her little ones go into the foster care system. People thought I was nuts for taking in three more kids, but I never thought twice about it.

Pam and I took a few road trips together the first one was to Juarez, Mexico along with my boyfriend Keith and Pam's husband. The day before we left on our trip, I lost my driver's license, so I brought a copy of my birth certificate for ID purposes with me. The three of them started teasing me since my last name was Sandoval. They kept telling me the Border Patrol was going to haul me off to a Mexican jail because I did not have a photo ID. I was really upset and started crying, they were acting so serious, and yet at the same time, they were laughing and enjoying themselves way too much.

On the same trip to Mexico, there were little kids in the streets begging for money. I started giving these little ones all my change and reaching for the dollar bills that I had. Pam kept telling me not to be giving my money to the kids, I asked her why, and she would point to the kid's mother in an expensive car. The kids were all dressed in rags with dirty little faces begging on the streets while their mother was waiting at the car for them. It did not matter to me, I could not resist those little eyes looking at me, and asking me "Pretty lady, pretty lady, pennies please?" Once again, Pam and the guys were teasing me only this time calling me a sucker.

On another trip, we drove to Wyoming, and we stopped to visit some of Pam's family in Canyon City, CO and then my dad's family in Denver. Pam got the biggest kick out my family and she told me "I have never met so many loving and loud people who when you walk in their house, you feel so welcomed and when you leave you are so full of great food."

One day I saw a mole on Pam's leg and asked her if she had been to the doctor to have it checked. The mole was small with jagged edges around the borders and black in color. I told her she needed to get it looked at and it did not look right to me at all. She kept telling me it was just an "Itty, bitty, ugly, mole." After a while, I called my doctor and made her an appointment. I then had to drag her to see him. The doctor took one look at the mole and excised it, along with a decent size portion of her leg. When the pathology report came back, it said that the mole had been cancerous. The doctor felt comfortable that he had removed it all, but he wanted her to come back for follow-up care just to be sure.

In the late winter of 1997, Pam and I drove to Tina's house in Oklahoma to pick up Shawna. Right as we were getting ready to head out, it started snowing hard. Tina and my son in law kept telling us we should not risk the drive back to Albuquerque and stay at their house until the storm passed. Pam kept insisting she needed to get home, and since she was from Colorado and had driven in snow her whole life, we would be okay. Pam had made up her mind and there was no changing it, so we headed out. About 40 miles after leaving Tina's, the roads were ice-packed, and we were only able to travel about 10 miles per hour while sliding all over the place. Because of the storm, we ended up stranded for three nights in Tucumcari, New Mexico, and another two nights at Pam's house in Moriarty, New Mexico.

One night while on this trip, Pam told me that she had an appointment with a specialist when we returned home. She had been having severe headaches and none of the medications she had been taking had been working, she admitted she was a little nervous but was tired of the pain. I knew she had been having headaches, but she had not let on to me how serious they had become.

A few days after returning home from our trip, Pam called and she was upset and crying. The specialist she had gone to see had ordered an MRI the same day of her appointment, and he had already read the results, and told her she would need to have surgery.

Pam told me that even though she and I had been best friends for many years at times her mom did not like me. Pam also said she had called her mom and dad to let them know what was going on and the date and time of her surgery. She made it clear she wanted all of us there and if her parents did not approve of her decision then they need not show up. I tried to tell her I would just wait for a call to get an update and she got angry with me and said "No, you will be there, got it Mik?"

The day of Pam's surgery, Shawna, my granddaughter Colette and I went to the hospital. After waiting what seemed like hours for the doctor, he finally came out. When I saw the look on his face, I knew the news was not going to be good. After explaining to us what he had found, Pam's sister asked the doctor what my friend's prognosis was, and he said that Pam was terminal. My heart sank. I stood up, excused myself, and ran to the hospital chapel. I started praying the rosary and crying so hard I could barely see through my tears.

I tried to compose myself the best I could I left the chapel and went to the cafeteria. While in the cafeteria, one of Pam's family members walked up to me and shook her finger in my face. She yelled, "Pam is not to know what the doctor said, do you understand this, Mikki? She is not to know, and if she finds out, you will have the wrath of me down your throat!" I just looked at her with tears streaming down my face and tried to give her a hug. I was not thinking about her outburst, rather the fact that we had just found out Pam was going to die. Confused and hurt, Shawna, Colette, and I left.

A few weeks passed and Pam and I had our daily talks,

but the subject of her surgery had not come up, it was as if we were evading the subject. I finally told my friend we needed to talk and after hanging up the phone, I drove up to Moriarty.

The drive to her house seemed endless and when I arrived, Pam was waiting for me. I walked in door sat down with my friend and I asked her "Pam do you want to know?" that is all I said and Pam answered, "I think I know, but tell me Mik." I took both of my friend's hands in mine, looked her in the eyes, and told her "Pam the doctor said the cancer has spread and it doesn't look good." We were crying and holding onto each other for dear life. After a while, Pam looked at me and said 'Mikki you are my best friend, it seems like you are the only one who respects and loves me enough to be totally honest, and I know how hard this has been for you." I looked at her in disbelief, Pam was worried about me, yet she was the one who was going through it all.

If Pam had asked the doctors about her condition, they would have had to tell her but in her heart she knew, and was hoping she would hear the words from someone who loved her. It was one of the hardest things I have ever had to do, was tell my best friend she was dying. It broke my heart, but I knew the friendship Pam and I had built for many years and I was not about to dishonor or disrespect it and I also knew she would have done the same for me.

I went out to my car and brought a gift in for her. She

opened the box and inside was a large clock; the clock had two red hearts intertwined with a picture of Jesus. When I gave it to her, I told her I felt that it represented over time how God had blessed our friendship.

As the months went by, Pam went through both chemotherapy and radiation treatments. After a while, her doctors in Albuquerque said there was nothing more they could do for my friend.

Pam's parents decided to take her out of state to another cancer treatment hospital in hopes of saving her life. Pam would call me when her parents would walk out of her hospital room and she would be crying and telling me she had had enough. I would tell her, she needed to tell her family that she did not want to continue but she finished that course of the treatments and returned home. After a short time, Pam called and told me her mom and dad wanted her to once again go back to the hospital she had just returned from. There had been no change in her test results, and she finally told her parents she was done with the treatments and that she had had enough.

One afternoon I drove up to Moriarty, when I got to Pam's house she was sitting on the couch and what I saw shocked me. She was so tiny and emaciated, I took one look at her and said, "Hey, Tweedy how are you?" She started laughing, and said "Thufferin Thucotash it's you, it's you." With almost all but a few wisps of her beautiful blond hair gone and her huge blue eyes along with her tiny frame, she looked just like that little bird. I kissed her on top of her head, smiled through my tears, and just about that time, I heard someone say, "How can you say things like that to her? You are so disrespectful Mikki." Pam looked over at this person and yelled back at them, "Mikki is allowing me to be me, she is the only one who is not walking on eggshells around me like everyone else, and so don't ever speak to her that way!"

With everyone having such a hard time accepting Pam's condition, in my opinion, some were not helping her to prepare for her final journey. I was trying to do what I could but it was extremely hard not being a family member and having a real say about anything. Pam had asked me to be her Medical Power of Attorney but I felt it should be a family member. I later regretted my decision for reasons I will not go into, but at the time, I felt it was for the best.

Pam and I were discussing hospice one afternoon as they were now in charge of her care. Out of nowhere one day she said, "Mik you could do this," I look at her and said, "Do what?" her reply was "Work in the hospice field." I looked at her and said, "Are you nuts woman?" She was laughing and told me "No, I really think you should. Mik, you have so much love in your heart and are very compassionate, just look what we are going through right now, I think you could really help people." I told her I would think about it but actually, I was thinking she had totally lost her mind.

One night while Pam was in the hospital I went to see

her. When I got there, her mom and dad were sitting with her and they looked so tired. I asked them if it would be okay if I stayed the night, because I knew they needed to go home and try to get some rest. I reassured her parents that I would not leave Pam's side, so they agreed and left the hospital. Pam had a very rough night; I stayed by her side, but I do not even know if she was aware that I was there. She ended up staying in the hospital a few days for that admission and was then sent home.

I received a call one evening from Pam's daughter Tara. She told me no one could get her mom calmed down and she asked me to come up to the house. When I arrived to the house, Pam was screaming and holding on to the side of her hospital bed, saying that she was falling. My friend was scared and agitated, and she kept fighting everyone. It was so hard to watch. Her family was frightened as well, and they were in such pain not knowing what to do. I climbed into her hospital bed, and I held my friend while gently rocking her and singing very softly to her. Pam finally calmed down, and when the ambulance arrived, they took her to the Hospice Unit at Anna Kaseman Hospital.

I believe that night she had a reaction to the medication she was taking. We thought we were going to lose Pam during this time, so I parked myself in the hospice unit, along with some of Pam's family members, and did not leave. Shawna came up a few times to the unit to say her goodbyes, and Jeremy called and told me what he wanted me to tell Pam. My kids' hearts were broken because they loved Pam so much. We all honestly thought this was the end, but after a few days, they moved Pam from the hospice unit to a nursing facility.

After her admission to the facility when I or certain other people would go visit her, Pam's parents would not leave her side. On one visit, I finally asked them if I could sit with my friend for a while and have some privacy. They agreed and left for some well-deserved time away. When Pam's parents left, she started getting upset and calling her mom names. I let her vent and then said to her "Sweetie, I know you are frustrated and mad. Your mom loves you and she is just trying to protect her little girl, and I am sure feels helpless like any mother would." "Try to imagine God forbid; it was one of your kids going through this." Pam got angry with me and said, "Why are you defending her Mik?" The way she has treated you at times why?" and then said, 'I know she loves me, but mom or dad will not even let me die the way I want or have the people I want around me." She told me that she was frustrated because they never talked about her dying. All I could do was listen and be there for my friend.

Every day after work and on the weekends, I would try to stop by to see Pam at the facility and spend as much time as I could with her. I would bring my Colette, who was three at the time, to visit her on some days. "Her Grandma Pam" she would call her. It was fall, and Colette, Pam and I would be sitting out on patio of the facility.

CAN I BORROW YOUR VACUUM?

Colette would gather little piles of leaves and toss them in the air, they would land on Pam and the two of them would let out the loudest giggles. Moments like these I was trying to hold on to.

Pam told me she wanted to be home and not at her parents' house if she was going to die. She had reiterated this several times to me and told me that she had discussed it with her parents as well. Pam loved her parents very much, but she wanted to be in her own bed and surrounded by the people and things she loved.

A few weeks passed, and the results of Pam's last MRI came in. Pam's parents decided to take her home to their place. When I asked what was going on, her parents would not tell me. All they would say was Pams condition had not changed, and they wanted to take her out of the facility, but I knew there was more to it than that.

After Pam went to her parents' house, whenever I would try to call her, people kept telling me she was sleeping. I am sure she was sleeping but not every time I called. When we finally did get to talk, Pam asked me, why I had not been calling every day. I reassured her that I had been trying to talk to her and then explained, what I had been told. The next thing I heard was Pam saying, "If Mikki calls put the call through to me, if I am sleeping wake me up, and if I don't talk to her every day I will know."

Approximately three weeks after Pam's parents took her out of the facility late one night my phone rang, and the call was from Pam's daughter Tara. She told me that her mom was not going to live through the night, and I needed to get up to her as soon possible. Tara also said, that her grandparents were saying that they did not want me to drive up to their house, that this was a time for their family and not outsiders. Tara told me to come up anyway as her mom had told her many times she wanted me there, and she and her brothers needed me. As badly as I wanted to jump in my car and get there, I could not, nor would I disrespect the wishes of Pam's parents while their daughter was dying. I told Tara her grandparents had the final say.

I was up all night praying, crying, and wishing I could be there with my friend, as well as support for her three kids. I had to work the next day, and as soon as I got to my desk and turned on my computer Tara called me once again, only this time she told me her mom had just died. Before we hung up Tara also said, "There is something you need to know, Mikki. You know the clock you gave Mom with the two hearts? Well mom always had to have it where she could see it. The last few days Mom's vision got worse, and she was frustrated because she could not see the numbers on the clock. We had to move it right next to her. Mikki, you need to know the last thing my mom looked at before she closed her eyes one last time was your clock."

I walked out into the hall, trying to control my tears, but my heart was breaking. I think, no matter how hard we try within our mind and heart, when someone we love dies, the pain is so deep we can never fully prepare ourselves for that moment. Since Pam's terminal diagnosis, I tried to prepare myself. I had imagined every scenario in my mind. I tried to picture what my feelings were going to be, or how I would react to the news of my friend's death. However, when the moment came it was nothing like that at all.

My supervisor had followed me out in the hall after my phone call from Tara and asked me what was wrong. I explained to her that my best friend had just died. She was very understanding and told me to go home but to have someone drive me. I did not want to be around anyone at that moment other than my family, so I left my office and drove straight to Shawna's work. I just needed some kind of validation. I cannot explain it, but I needed to hold onto my life, at that moment in time.

When I walked into Shawna's work, she took one look at me and knew what had happened. I went over and picked up my Colette and I held her tightly. Colette was just a little one and was squirming to go play, but she hugged me tightly and whispered in her little voice, "It's okay, Grandma, it will be okay." Shawna held and comforted me, and she said something to me which I will never forget. With her arms around me, she said, "Mom, Pam had her family, her friends, and people who were in her life. But Mom, you were her compassion for over 20 years – no one else Mom, only you!" Those words that my 22-year-old daughter said to me on that day is what got me through those darkest hours when I missed my friend so badly.

My best friend Pamela Tate died at the young age of 40 after a brave battle against malignant melanoma (skin cancer) that metastasized to her brain and other organs. It all started from one "Itty, bitty, ugly mole" on her leg. *I love you, I miss you, and I will never forget you girl!*

During Pam's memorial service, one of the questions the minister asked her kids is what they would remember most about their mom. Tara stood up and said, "The one thing I will remember about my mom is she and Mikki always on the phone for hours and hours, laughing, crying or just talking, and nobody ever getting it, but the two of them.

8

Was It All a Lie?

Mark and I met when he was 22, and I was 32 years old. My friend Melinda and I were joining a few friends for a night out. We pulled up into the parking lot of the bar and Melinda's friend Gary was there along with his friend Mark. I was meeting up with my friend Kevin for a drink that night and he was already at the bar so we all started playing pool and relaxing. Mark came over to join us, and Kevin seemed to be getting a little annoyed. Kevin and I had only been out to dinner once and another time to play pool so our relationship was in no way serious. Kevin had walked outside and while he was away, Mark asked me for my phone number, I wrote my number down and handed him the paper, but never expected him to call. When Kevin returned to the table, he did not like the fact that Mark was hanging out with us so he left.

Mark offered to drive me home, but I told him I came

with Melinda, so I was going to leave with her. So instead, he followed us back to my house. When Melinda dropped me off in front of my house, Mark and I sat in my driveway and talked for hours. He was friendly and charming, and the fact he was so cute certainly was a plus.

Kevin called the next morning, we had talked about going to the Drag Races a few weeks before, and that morning I had totally forgot about the conversation we had about doing this. When he called to confirm, I thanked him but told him I actually did not feel like going. As soon as I hung up the phone it rang again, only this time it was Mark. He said was in the neighborhood, and wanted to see if he could stop by.

Mark and I started spending a lot of time together and before too long, we were living together. I was renting a spacious, beautiful house and had a roommate at the time, but right before Mark moved in my roommate decided to move to California so it was just Mark, and I and the kids.

Mark and I were married on April 29, 1989 we decided to stay apart the night before to have some tradition in our wedding. We finally saw one another as I walked up the isle to the gazebo in Old Town where our ceremony took place. I wore the Chantilly lace-wedding gown that Mark's mom wore when she married his dad many years before. My son Jeremy gave me away, and my daughters stood up with me while Mark's brother played the guitar. Old Town is a popular tourist attraction in the heart of Albuquerque.

People would stop us from different parts of the world, and ask to take our picture, as they had never seen a wedding in a gazebo. It was an unforgettable day.

After the ceremony, our friends had a reception for us at the bar we met at, and then we were off for our fantastic wedding night. For one of our wedding gifts Mark's parents and brother reserved a night for us, in the honeymoon suite at the hotel his brother worked at. It was a beautiful suite with a bar, Jacuzzi and many other amenities. Marks brother and Tina also surprised us by decorating the room with rose petals and personal touches to make it even more memorable.

The next morning, we woke up to a phone call to get home because Tina was in labor. We timed Tina's labor pains Sunday and Sunday night. I used to tease Mark and tell him that he went from being single to being a dad and being Papa (grandpa) all within two days.

On May 1, 1989, my beautiful grandson Jonathon Gregory made his entrance into this world. Tina and Jonathon were both having complications, so Tina asked me to go with the baby down to the Neonatal Intensive Care Unit. In the meantime, Mark stayed and held Tina's hand until I went back into the delivery room.

Six months after we were married Mark and I decided to renew our vows in the Catholic Church. During this time, we were required to attend classes, but first we had to take a compatibility test. Even though we were married in a civil ceremony, the church did not recognize the marriage. We took the test, which had over a hundred questions. Father Jim called us into his office, and told us we had only missed one question each, and since we were already married in a civil ceremony and living together for the past six months, he did not think we needed the classes. Mark and I looked at one another and in our minds and hearts; Father Jim only validated what we already knew. Father Jim did want talk to each of us privately about any concerns we had before the ceremony, but other than that, we were free to marry.

Our renewal of vows took place at St. Bernadette's Catholic Church. I had always loved this church and attended Mass there when I was young. I still believe it is one of the most beautiful churches around. We decorated the church with candles and flowers and that night I walked up the aisle on my son's arm to *Ave Maria*. The ceremony was beautiful and my heart was overflowing with happiness and love.

When Mark and I first met I would drink occasionally, we would go out dancing and enjoy ourselves. After a while, if both of us were drinking for some reason we would fight, so I decided I was not going to drink anymore. Our first ten years of marriage we had our ups and downs as most married couples do but we were happy. Around our 11th year of marriage, things started to go downhill rapidly. I kept asking myself, how two people who had always promised each other to keep the lines of communication open, were now watching as the lines fell down around them. There were also things that certainly should not have taken place within our marriage that I was gradually finding out.

Mark was working out of town for months at a time, he had a terrific job, and I was supportive and encouraged him. While he was out of town, some things happened that I just could not get over. In addition, I had been around alcohol my entire life and it was starting to take over our life, our family, and our marriage. The problem had been there all along, but I just did not want to accept it.

I have always believed Mark that had a good heart, and I never doubted that, but as time progressed I was starting to fall out of love with him for many different. After a while, I started to stay in our spare room. At first I told him it was because of his snoring, but it is where I slept for the next two years. I just could not keep up the pretense any longer.

I talked to some of our family members, and Father Jim in hopes of getting some help. I attended Al-anon meetings, which did not go over well with Mark. I begged, pleaded, cried, and even gave Mark ultimatums. My attempts to get him to stop drinking just seemed to go nowhere so I left him. The way I left might not have been the best way to go about it. However, something needed to change.

Mark and I remained legally married for twenty years and separated for the last seven of our marriage. We only saw each other a few times in person during our separation.

SHATTERED PIECES, LOVING HEART

Mark would not file the paperwork for the divorce since I am the one who left. I had prepared the paperwork myself, and it sat in my file cabinet for several years. I am not sure why I kept it for so long, but I finally was ready to get the divorce finalized. I met Mark at my bank, we signed the papers together, notarized them and I filed and paid for the divorce. The court waived the waiting period and five days later, our divorce was final.

Mark and I remained friends for a few years by email or chatting occasionally. I truly believed we would always be friends, until last summer. Even though Mark and I are divorced, he admitted something to me that in my opinion was the ultimate betrayal. I felt he had not only betrayed me but also other people who were important to me and he was keenly aware of this. I had my suspicions of this very thing happening many years before when he and I were what I believed to be happily married. I had questioned him about it throughout the years, and what I had suspected, but he always denied it. By his admitting to me what was going on, it started me thinking about how much of our marriage had been a lie. I thought about what he told me for a while and then I then sat down and wrote to him and the other person involved, said what I needed to say to the both of them and finally closed this chapter in my life.

9

Shattered Trust

In the summer of 2000, I started talking to a man named Peter who is from Canada. We started talking online and on the phone pretty often. Things with Mark had been going downhill for a quite a long time. Besides the obvious alcohol abuse, he had betrayed and lied to me about things and I felt trapped, helpless, and alone in our marriage.

Peter and I became close, and in October 2000, we met out of state. He and I became even closer that weekend. The day I got back to Albuquerque I told Mark I was leaving. Living with one man and thinking of another was not right. The way I left was not the right way to go about it and I realized this later on, but I did know I had to leave.

This new man had given me the courage to do just that. Peter and I talked on the phone for hours each night and on the weekends. We traveled back and forth between

Canada and New Mexico over the next nine months. I was happy and felt so in love with this amazing, charming, and beautiful French Canadian. Peter had a son, who was almost 18 and a best friend Carl. During my visits to Canada and on the phone, we had all become great friends.

I was planning a trip to Canada in February for Valentine's Day and it was Carl's birthday on February 15, so we decided would celebrate it all at once. Peter picked me up at SeaTac Airport in Seattle Tacoma WA and then we drove the rest of the way to Abbotsford where his apartment was.

The first night of my trip was great, for Valentine's Day Peter had a huge stuffed velvet dog with a big heart that hung off its neck that said, "I love you" for me. He also gave me a beautiful heart necklace and I was on top of the world. The next day we went to the mall, he took me out to lunch to a beautiful Canadian restaurant on the water. It started to snow and I was catching snowflakes on my tongue and picking up tiny maple leaves in the park it was truly a magical time.

On February 15th, Carl's birthday, we decided to go to a few clubs to celebrate. I did not drink alcohol, so I drake 7 Up instead. We met up with a few couples that Peter and Carl knew who I had met before and we were enjoying our night. We arrived back to Peter's apartment and then walked a few doors down to Carl's place. I got up to use the restroom and when I sat back down, I took a few drinks of my water. Within a short time, I started to feel very strange. I excused myself, and Peter had his son walk me back to his apartment, because by this time I could barely stand up.

The last thing I remember clearly is Peter trying to take my clothes off in front of his son. I was crying and begging him to stop; he called me a baby and told me to shut up, and if I did not like it to get out. I must have passed out because the next thing I can remember was people on top of me, one after the other. I could see shadows and I would begin to feel something and then blacked out again. I am not sure how long this went on nor am I clear of all the details of what happened that night.

I woke up the next day with my clothes disheveled, and I knew something was terribly wrong. I had bruises and teeth marks all over my body. I was bleeding from parts of my body I should not have been and there were other things going on as well. Since I was in a foreign country, I did not know what to do.

I took my cell phone into the bathroom and called my eldest daughter Tina. I was crying hysterically while trying to be quiet at the same time. I ran the water in the tub and sink hoping Peter and his son could not hear what I was saying to her. I told Tina what had happened. Her response was, "Are you sure, mom?" I said, "Yes honey I think so, I think so!" I believe I was still in some sort of denial and shock, yet at the same time, *I knew it happened*. When I came out of the bathroom, Peter started asking me questions about my phone call. I just played it off the best I could that I was sick, I wanted to call Tina, and did not want to interrupt his hockey game on TV.

I had one more night to stay at his house and I was too afraid to eat anything the rest of that day or night. When it was time for bed, I did not close my eyes even for a minute I just laid there and silently prayed to myself. My flight was very early in the morning, and we had to be at the airport two hours early for security and with the two-hour drive back to the airport, we left around 5:30 am.

When I got into Peter's truck, the fear I felt was almost debilitating for the ride. Neither of us said one word to each other the whole time. With each passing mile marker on the highway, I would say a prayer giving thanks that I was okay. It was the longest ride of my life. When we arrived at the airport, I asked Peter to drop me off out front. Neither of us said goodbye and I got my luggage out of his truck and did not look back. I kept entirely to myself throughout the three-hour flight back home. I did not move or make eye contact with anyone. I was just a scared person staring out the window of the plane who did not know what to do, think, or feel.

My friend Barb picked me up at the airport back in Albuquerque, she tried to give me a welcome back hug, and when she reached for me, I jumped back. She asked me if I was okay, and wanted to know what had happened, but I did not want talk about it. I kept quiet and did not say a word all the way home except that I was tired from the trip. Barb told me when I talked to her about it sometime later that she knew when she saw me on that day that something horrible had happened.

When I got to my apartment, I went into my bedroom, laid down on my floor, curled in a fetal position, and cried until I had no more tears. I then drove myself to the urgent care center, and they did what they needed to do and they contacted the Rape Crisis Center for me. Shawna and I were sharing an apartment during this time, and the next time I saw her I told her what had happened. She kept telling me how sorry she was that I was hurting so much, and how much she loved me. At one point, I remember putting my head on Shawna's lap and crying as she brushed my tears away while telling me, "Mom it will be okay, it will, and I am so sorry you are in so much pain." Knowing my daughter had to see me this way, was one of the hardest things for me. I only wish she knew what a tremendous strength she was and how she did help me.

It took me longer to tell Jeremy, as I knew his reaction would be of anger and wanting to try to get even with the men who had done this to his mom. Jeremy is my only son and has always been extremely protective of me since he was a little boy. "No one better hurt or mess with my mom, no one!" he used to say. When I finally was able to tell him about what had happened, it was just as I thought it would be. It took his girlfriend and me a while to convince him not to get in his car, drive to Canada, and shoot the animals that had hurt me. I have never forgotten the pain and anger I saw in my son's eyes on that day.

Mark's reaction was different. I made the mistake of telling him about what had happened to me. Even though we were not together, we were still friends. His reaction was both anger at the men for hurting me and he was blaming me as well. He told me had I not put myself in the position, and gone to Canada it never would of have happened, and it was my fault. Years later Mark would still blame me, and bring it up whenever we would talk. I think he was still upset because I left him, more than it was a personal attack on me, but the words cut so deep.

A week or so after this all happened. Peter called me one night and he was extremely drunk. I could hear his friend Carl in the background. Carl made the remark to me as he always did, "You know you want me girl," it was a joke with him or so I thought. My answer would always be, "Dream on buddy." I did not say anything back, and he again yelled, "You know you want me." Once again, there was silence at my end of the phone. Then he yelled out where I could hear him loud and clear, "Well you may not think you want me, but the last time you were here, I got the best birthday present of all. We all had a great time taking turns with you, and man you were good!" Carl was laughing in the background and then he yelled out, "Thanks, Peter, for giving her to us; it's the gift that keeps on giving, and what a present we all had with you girl, right Peter?" Peter kept swearing and kept yelling at Carl to keep his mouth shut, and tried to silence him. I could not believe I was hearing this. I felt paralyzed while at the same time my mind was screaming *"Oh, my God! Oh, my God! It happened! It did happen!* "I threw the phone down, started getting very dizzy, went to the bathroom, and got so sick I thought I would never gather my composure again. I went back to my room and lay down on my floor. I continue to go to the bathroom get sick and then back to my room for what seemed like hours while trying to process it all. I did not know what to do, how to react, what to feel, what had they all done to me, how many had done whatever to me. My mind was spinning, and the rest of me could not keep up. I felt dirty, ashamed, and alone and scared.

The test results did end up showing that several different men had raped me, and I had been given a date rape drug. When I went back to the Rape Crisis Center, my counselor told me that it would be extremely difficult if not impossible to prosecute the men who had done this to me. Since they had given me a date rape drug and I was in another country at the time it occurred, the District Attorney's office did not want to pursue my case but there would be a report filed. I looked at the counselor in disbelief, thanked her for her hard work and compassion, and walked out feeling violated once again.

I received counseling through the Rape Crisis Center and through the Employee Assistant Program where I worked and throughout the years, if I have felt I needed to talk to someone. One of the hardest things, I still deal with at times are called triggers. When I finally learned what they were and how to deal with them it has helped. Occasionally a situation can arise which will bring up a memory, feeling, smell, or a noise, which can bring on a panic attack. It has only happened to me a few times but I do know what the triggers are now and how to handle the situation if needed.

It has been almost 10 years since that horrific night. My counselor told me it is probably good that I cannot remember the details of that happened to me. At first, I was upset because not knowing the details of what all they had done to me, for how long, were there even more than Peter, his son and Carl who hurt me, along with other questions that haunted me. My memory loss was due to the drug they gave me, but my counselor also told me that when our mind blocks details of a trauma like what I went through, our survival and coping mechanism kick in. This is the brain's way of protecting us, and I truly am thankful.

I had to learn how to forgive the men for the horrible things they did to me. I was able to do this through my faith in God, the love, and support I have in my life and the wonderful counselors who worked with me. It was not an easy process at all and has taken years of hard work to be able to get to this point. It does not mean I forgot, because believe you me I have not, nor will I ever, but I could not carry the hurt, anguish and pain that was in my heart. I believe it would have been too self-destructive for me, and I refuse to remain a victim of those sick individuals who hurt me.

10

Stupidity, Fear and Embarrasment

In January 2004, I had been experiencing some health problems for quite a while but ignoring them out of stupidity, fear, and embarrassment. Out of fear, because when I was 22 years old I had to have a complete hysterectomy due to cancer. Out of embarrassment, because the symptoms I was having were things I did not want to talk about and share with people. Out of stupidity because I kept putting off going to the doctor.

Besides having bleeding and losing weight rapidly, whenever I ate something even a bite of a cracker my stomach would double over in pain. I finally went to the doctor, and he ordered the dreaded colonoscopy. I had put it off and always seem to find an excuse not to have it done, but I knew it was time. Anyone who has had a colonoscopy, I am sure will agree with me the preparation for it is no fun whatsoever. My doctor had me drink a gallon of a laxative solution over a two-hour period; and then I placed myself right next to the bathroom for hours.

The next day, Shawna drove me to have the test done. I put on a gown; they inserted an IV, gave me something to help relax me, and wheeled me into the procedure room, after a few minutes I was asleep.

During the procedure, I woke up several times and I remember saying things like "ouch, that hurts" as well as a few curse words. I would then hear the doctor say to give me more medication. This I came to find out, was not because they had not medicated me well enough, but because of how many polyps I had and the different locations throughout my colon my doctor had to go to remove them.

While in the recovery room, the doctor came in and told Shawna and I, from what he had found he was going to refer me to a surgeon and he felt the sooner the better. He said that my kids also needed to have a colonoscopy done as well. My doctor said we would know more when the pathology report came back, but from what he saw, it did not look very good.

The surgeon's office called me a few days later and we scheduled an appointment for a consultation. I knew immediately when I met Doctor L. that he was someone I would be able to trust. Doctor L. is a vascular surgeon who has performed some remarkable surgeries in the Albuquerque area, and his reputation is impeccable. I was scared, but the doctor made me feel at more at ease. After going over my test results with me and talking to me at great length, Dr. L told me that I did indeed need to have surgery and he would know more after he opened me up.

When I got back to my office at the Department of Energy, a few of my coworkers who knew I had the appointment was waiting for me. They were comforting and encouraging, but they also saw my fear. My friend Melissa and I had become very good friends at work we always took our breaks and lunch together and we would hang out outside of work as well. Melissa kept me upbeat and as optimistic as possible during this time. Melissa could always make me laugh and smile; she truly was a good friend. My family and friends were very optimistic and supportive during this time. A close friend of mine Jeff who lives in Flagstaff, Arizona, was very sweet and he called me every night, he sent plants and flowers and he mailed me CD's he had made for me to help me relax.

I had re-written my advance directive, living will, and power of attorney during this time. With tears coming out of our eyes just thinking if something went wrong, Shawna and I went over her copy of the papers two nights before my surgery. I am sure that it must have been very difficult for her to do this, but I do not want my kids to have to wonder or to go through any more stress than necessary. I also do not want to put them in a position to have to make those kinds of decisions, if and when the time comes.

The night before my surgery, I had to prep of course.

SHATTERED PIECES, LOVING HEART

It was not like having a colonoscopy but totally cleaning out my entire system. Five days before surgery I could only have clear liquids and the night before of course clean out my bowels. My older sister Judy drove in from Amarillo that night, which meant so much to me.

Shawna drove me to the hospital the day of my surgery and my daughter in law Cindy and my sister were waiting for us. Tina was in Oklahoma awaiting word, we decided she would fly out to help me when I was home after the surgery.

Shawna and I were in the pre-op area talking and I look up at the clock, and the next thing I remember I was in the elevator with my doctor. My doctor said surgery went well but he had to take out 17 lymph nodes, and they did not look good to him, and then I fell back to sleep.

While in the hospital, my doctor ordered a PCA Demerol pump for me. I have had major surgeries before, and pain medications and I do not go well together. Not only do I have anaphylactic reactions to many medications but also I am ultra-sensitive to them. When the nurses brought me from recovery to my hospital room, I had a nasogastric (Ng-tube) and a few other things connect to me. I hated the Ng-tube and I kept begging the nurses and doctor to remove it.

The next night of my admission, I asked the nurse if he could please turn the free flowing medication off on the PCA pump, but leave on just the button to where I could push it to get a shot of the medication if I needed it. The night nurse did just that, and I was able to get just enough pain relief and was comfortable. In the morning when the nurse on duty came in my room, she turned the free flow on again to the pump. I asked her several times and explained the best I could, that it was just too much medication for me, but she refused to turn the dosage down. The nurse kept saying I needed the full amount o pain medication because of the type of surgery that I had. After going back and forth with her, I finally told the nurse to take me off the pump and to give me *Extra Strength Tylenol* for my pain. After all of my surgeries, except for one in 1978 with my diagnosis of cancer, I would go off pain medication after 24 to 48 hours. My kids would get angry with me because they did not like seeing their mom in pain. Nevertheless, the anaphylactic reactions or drug sensitivities I have experienced were not worth it to me.

My son Jeremy hates hospitals and it was very hard for him to come and visit me, and when he and my daughter in law Cindy came and spent some time with me, it really lifted my spirits. I remember when Jeremy walked in the room; I had the biggest smile because I knew how hard it was for him. He had told me several years before this surgery, when I had a triple bone fusion done in my back, that it was just extremely hard for him to see his mom lying in a hospital bed.

Shawna came up every day, and her boyfriend Jon came up to visit as well; it was so sweet. Jon's mom who was a nurse would come to the hospital and sit with me, and if she saw, I was getting over tired she would tell my visitors they needed to leave unless they were family and I was very grateful to her for this. I am the type of patient if someone comes to see me I feel I have to stay awake and visit with him or her. Melissa and some of my co-workers had gotten together and brought me a card with donations from work. They told me they knew I would be out for quite a while and wanted to make sure I would be okay financially. I will never forget their kindness and generosity.

On the third night of my admission, the nurse came to check the suction on my Ng tube and said she needed to page the doctor right away, which is when I started to panic. Blood was filling the suction canister much faster than it should have been. This happen around 11:00 p.m. and my first reaction were to get on the phone and call Tina in Oklahoma. Tina talked to both the nurse and the doctor and asked them if she needed to get to Albuquerque, the doctor told her to get there as soon as she could. He explain to the both of us that it look as though they were going to have to take me back to surgery because they thought I might have internal bleeding. Once Tina told me she was catching a flight to Albuquerque, I calmed down and I somehow knew it would be all right. When my daughter arrived from Oklahoma and was by my side, within a short time the bleeding starting to slow down therefore, I did not have to go back to surgery.

I stayed in the hospital one more day and then went

home all stapled up. When admitted to the hospital, my doctor said my expected stay would be 10-14 days, not this girl. I was an inpatient for four days, which is what my average stay has been regardless of the reason. I always tell them, get me in, get whatever done, and get me out. I just seem to heal much better at home.

My doctor performed a sub-total colectomy and took out sections from all over my colon, and as he put it "Re-attach, and sewed me back together in pieces" A total of 52 inches was removed which left me with eight inches of colon. He also removed 17 lymph nodes. The pathology report showed all of the lymph nodes were non-cancerous, but out of the polyps and sections of my colon that was removed, there were several malignancies and some precancerous as well. The cancer had not spread beyond the bowel wall and once again, the Good Lord had his arms around me.

I have been cancer free for almost seven years now. So please, if you are reading this get your test done when you reach the age when you should have a baseline colonoscopy, or are having any symptoms, or if there is a history of colon cancer in your family, no matter how embarrassing it may seem, or how frightened you may be. Because of my stupidity, fear and embarrassment, things could have ended very differently for me.

11

Paradise

I was living in Oklahoma, staying with my daughter Tina and her family after having undergone an unexpected surgery. I had been applying for jobs everywhere when I received a job offer for a position with a government contractor at Thule Air Force Base, in Greenland. My daughter-in-law Cindy and I drove to Colorado Springs so I could get the paperwork started and my security clearance reinstated.

Shortly after returning home from Colorado Springs, I received an e-mail from the Administrator of a hospital that I had submitted my resume to months before. This job was with another Department of Defense contractor, which was located on a tropical island in the middle of the South Pacific. The island is two and one half miles long and three-quarters of a mile wide. It is the Ronald Reagan Ballistic Missile Defense Test Site otherwise known as

RTS, which is located on Kwajalein Atoll in the Marshall Islands. The Marshall Islands are approximately half way between, Hawaii and Australia. She asked me if I was still interest in the position that I had applied for as a Medical Billing Specialist, and I told her that I was.

We emailed back and forth, and then she said that she wanted to set up an interview for me with my prospective supervisor CB. When I interviewed with CB, I knew I wanted the job. She made me feel completely at ease. After the interview, I was excited and felt it went well. CB told me they had more candidates to interview, and I thought to myself, there was no way I was going to get this kind of opportunity, things like this just did not happen to me. Well a few weeks later, I received the call and they offered me the position in the Marshall Islands. I was excited beyond words and just could not believe it.

Human Resources completed my background check, verified my references, and then received a green light from the Chief Medical Officer of the hospital for my physical competence. I then received an email from Teresa Bell, who was tremendously helpful. She walked me through every step of the process, which included the movers coming to pack my belongings, getting my airline tickets and receiving my government orders. I already had a valid passport so I did not have to wait the six weeks or longer getting one.

For some reason I kept forgetting where I was going, and could not pronounce the name of this little island. I kept asking my son-in-law and daughter every few hours, "Now where am I going?" They would laugh and tell me "Kwajalein Mom, Kwajalein!"

My oldest daughter Tina had been working as a federal police officer for many years at the base here in Oklahoma. She had talked about a new military officer, who started working in her office. She said she noticed he was extremely tanned and she knew he could not of transferred from somewhere around here. She just came out and said to him one day, "Sir, you sure are tanned," and he told her he had just come from Kwajalein in the Marshall Islands. She mentioned I would be starting a new job there, and he told Tina he would be happy to talk to me if I had any questions. I did go in with her to talk with him, and he gave me a much better picture of where I was going and what to expect. We live in a very small world sometimes. First, I had never heard of this place and now all of a sudden I am going to work and live there, and my daughter knows someone who had just moved back from there.

I received a call from Albuquerque that there had been a serious family emergency. I flew to Albuquerque, spent six days there so I could help where I possibly could and then I flew back to Oklahoma on Sunday. The next day the movers arrived for my pack out. I had no idea what to take. I was packing bottled water, salad dressings I loved, my set of dishes, pots, and pans – you name it, I packed it. My son-in-law, who had been in the military for over 20 years got the biggest kick out me, and kept saying 'Mom, they do have water I am sure, and everything you will need, you will probably be living in single quarters." I did not listen to him and he would laugh and tease me about it, and of course, it turns out, he was right.

Three days later, it was time to leave. There were many tears at the airport when I said goodbye, tears flowed from Lawton to Dallas TX, Dallas to Honolulu HI, and Honolulu to Kwajalein. My kids and I had never been any further than a nine-hour drive away from each other. When I stepped off the plane onto the tarmac, I took one look around and caught my breath, saying to myself I can do this! What a spectacular site. Never in my wildest dreams could I imagine such a beautiful place; it astounded me. To think that I would be living and working there it just boggled my mind.

They have many procedures in place when you land on Kwajalein, because it is a secure military base. I was taken to a room for a short briefing, and in the meantime, the police and their K-9 dogs were checking everyone's luggage and personal belongings for bombs and drugs. When the briefing was complete, a coworker and the hospital administrator were waiting to welcome me. I arrived tired, jet lagged but very excited.

The time difference took some adjustment. Kwajalein is 17 hours later than Central time, and our workweeks were Tuesday through Saturday to coincide with CONUS (Continental Unites States). My coworker drove me around and showed me the island, which only took a short time since the island is small. The only transportation other than government or hospital vehicles, are either bicycles or golf carts. It cracked me up to find out that we could rent a golf cart periodically.

My co-worker then took me by my BQ (Bachelor Quarters) which I would call home for the next 2 years. For those who are unaccompanied status or by themselves they live in BQ's. Married employees live in military style housing. I loved my BQ; it had cute rattan furniture and was perfect for living on an island. There was a welcome basket waiting for me in my room, what a thoughtful touch that was to me. My things from Oklahoma were going to take, on the average, two months to get there by barge. My supervisor had advised me to mail ahead whatever personal things I might need until my shipment came in. I did not have a television of course but one of my new neighbors saw us driving up, and he offered me the use of a TV and helped carry my luggage up to the second floor for me. I was pretty darn impressed with the friendliness already.

My company had already set up my APO box and phone number before I arrived on the island, which of course I thought that was great. On a whim, I decided to go check my mailbox that first day, and it was such a surprised to see there were cards in there from my Tina. It meant so much to me. She knows her mom, and knew how much I would be missing all of them. I went back to my BQ, rested up for a few minutes, and walked outside.

SHATTERED PIECES, LOVING HEART

As soon as I reached the end of the steps, I heard the thickest Boston accent coming out of this woman standing by the BQ. We introduced ourselves, her name was Robbie; she also work at the hospital as the Lab supervisor. Robbie and I were next-door neighbors and she had just arrived a few days before me. Robbie is a character, and she tells it like it is. She is crazy as all get out, fun to be around and has one of the biggest hearts of anyone I know. I did not know what to think at first. The weird thing is that two weeks after we had become friends Robbie started calling me Mish. There was no way she could have known that my younger brothers and sisters have called me Mish or Mishi ever since we were little. I knew at that moment that Robbie and I were destined to be friends.

Robbie and I had an invitation to Lexy Galloway's family BBQ that night. Lexy and her entire family were so nice and made me feel right at home. Lexy became one of my closest friends, she has a remarkable outlook on life and the sweetest heart. On Kwajalein, there is always a BBQ, a party on the beach or just a get together. What amazed me, is just about everyone was so friendly, warm, and welcoming.

All along the beach, on both sides of the island there are benches like those that you see at bus stops in the states every so often. One was about 50 feet from the hospital where Robbie and I worked at, and 150 feet from our BQ building. Robbie and I dubbed this '*the crying bench*' (which is actually the picture for the cover of this book) We would sit at the crying bench if we needed to talk, gripe, or when we were sad, we would cry our hearts out and all was better. On the anniversary of my rapes, the healing process was almost complete and Robbie knew it was an extremely intense day for me. After work, she and I went to our bench, she then handed me a bunch of rocks and picked up some for herself. Robbie then told me in that demanding Boston accent "Okay Mish, start talking, throwing, and let it out!" She and I were yelling, crying, and at the same time just throwing rocks at the sorry, sick people who had hurt me. The pain and the feelings were just pouring out of me and hitting the ocean; it was extremely cathartic. Thank you so much, my friend!

One evening, I was sitting on the curb outside of my BQ; all of a sudden, I see this coconut walking by. I kid you not it was a big coconut, and it was walking by me. I looked and looked again, and then I let out a scream. People came running out of the BQ buildings to see what had happened. One of the Kwajalein police officers just happen to be riding by on his bike; everyone start laughing, the officer told me it was just a coconut crab. I had never in my life heard of such a thing. The officer took the crab and tossed it away from me, which I was grateful. In addition to the "walking coconuts," I would also see tiny seashells walking along the beach or near my feet when I was sitting on the crying bench. I know they were crabs, but being a city girl, I had never seen such sights.

SHATTERED PIECES, LOVING HEART

For my birthday, my friend Robbie threw me a party. I was so excited, many people showed up and I had only been on the island for three months. It truly made my heart smile. It was a terrific time my first island party wow! I remember hearing people say, "Bring a Pupu platter." I had no idea what they meant. I will not go into what I was thinking they meant, but I am sure you can imagine. Once again, I had the island in stitches I then found out that a Pupu platter is a bunch of different appetizers on one plate.

I would like to discuss some of the wonderful people I met while on the island. Of course, it would take a book in itself to name them all but here are a few. I had not touched alcohol for 17 years before I went to Kwajalein and did not, for the first 8 months after I arrived. Then one night I got a wild hair and decided I was going to drink and my drink of choice was kamikazes or should I say several. For someone who had not touched alcohol for such a long time I got very drunk. My friend Dan, walked me across the street to my BQ, and made sure I made it in okay. Thanks Dan!

The next weekend, a group of us went back to the club. My friend Cathy Williams told the bartender "Do not and I repeat do not, give this woman kamikazes." Well of course, when she was not looking I ordered one. The next thing I know she is chasing me all over the bar yelling at me, "No, drop that kamikaze woman" it was hilarious. She knew I was not a drinker, and after the weekend before she was not about ready to let her friend get drunk again. I drank on weekends for about 6 weeks, I would go out and have a few beers, but after the 6 weeks, I went back to drinking only water. During the short time, I did drink people would tease me about having a beer in my hand. Cathy is a terrific person who listens and keeps everyone laughing; she is a true friend. I am thankful not only for our time on Kwajalein but she has remained a very dear friend to this day. By the way, Cathy, you are always right, with the exception of "No, beer is not food woman!"

I met my friend Susannah at the Pit (which is another name for the Ocean View Club) through Robbie. Susannah is the sweetest person, when she smiles, she lights up an entire room. She has a presence about her that is so natural and down to earth. I ended up moving into the same BQ building as she lived. Everyone loves Susannah, she is smart beyond her years, and I use to tell her she is an old soul because of her youth, and worldly knowledge. Susannah would invite me over and we would listen to relaxing music, do facials, and just have a girl's night. In the evenings, you would find us outside on the balcony just chatting away.

Another one of the women I had the pleasure of getting to know is Janet. She arrived on the island a few months after I did and she and I worked together at the hospital. I call Janet a North Carolina true southern belle. Janet is great. I would go to her office if I needed to escape and she always had a hug, a laugh, or an ear willing to listen to me. If a problem would arise at work, Janet was the one I would turn to for help. Between the two of us, we could always come up with a solution. She and I love classic rock, so whenever there was classic rock playing on the island you would usually find us there. Thank you, Janet for being such a good friend and doing it with such class.

My friend Dixie that I had come to know is such a good woman. Dixie was one of our DJ's on the island for the Armed Forces Radio Station. She is down to earth and has such a loving heart. She and I would have countless hours of heart to heart talks. She really understood some things that I had been through, or was going through while I was on the island. I had to fly home back to the states unexpectedly and Dixie stepped up to represent me as co-chair for the American Cancer Society's Relay for Life Cancer Walk. I am extremely grateful that she did this on my behalf. Dixie is a very special person, and she always makes me feel like I have the ability to do whatever I need to accomplish.

During orientation, we had the opportunity to take a boat over to the third world island Ebeye. During this trip, I met Renee Hirn and her family. They are an example of what we should all strive to be. Renee is a nurse, and her husband is a high-ranking official in the military. Their daughter reminds me so much of my granddaughter Colette. At 11 years old, I saw Renee's daughter organizing all kinds of community projects. I wish more of our youth had that kind of attitude. The Hirn family works within the community helping others because it is the right thing to do. I was lucky enough to house sit for Renee whenever her family would go on Temporary Assignment somewhere else or (TDY) in military terms. I had the greatest time, and it was delightful to be in a real house, have room to walk and move about. I was able to cook on a real stove again and what a treat that was. They had a bathtub that I was able to use. I missed having a tub so much, and Renee was so sweet, there was always a gift basket for me with bath luxuries waiting when I would housesit. She also had a dog-named Boomer he and I had the best time together and would go for long walks along the beach; Boomer was one of my all-time favorite dog-friends. Renee and her family are always so welcoming and they genuinely care about others.

I would also like to say thank you to the people I worked with at Kwajalein Hospital, which include the CMO, the doctors, the Psychologist on staff, Administrator, CNP, all of the nurses, lab technicians, radiologists, front desk people, medical records person, workman's compensation ladies, pharmacist's, and the Marshallese employees. Each of you is the epitome of wonderful caregivers and great people in general. It was truly a privilege and honor to work with each one of you. In addition, I would like to extend a very special thanks to my first supervisor. Thank you for hiring me and bringing me on to the island, which allow me to be a part of the wonderful team at the hospital.

Scuba diving is a huge thing on Kwajalein. They say it is one of the best places in the world to dive. Robbie and

SHATTERED PIECES, LOVING HEART

I took classes to get scuba certified. I did well, and passed the written test, made it to the pool, which is the first step before going on an actual dive in the ocean. I attempted twice in the pool, with all my scuba equipment on, but I began getting extremely claustrophobic and uncomfortable. I could feel myself starting to panic so I never was certified.

Snorkeling, I was able to do quite a bit. I am by no means the strongest swimmer, which made it a little challenging living on an island surrounded by water. Robbie use to tease me and try to get me to go out further in the ocean like she and others would. However, there again I was a little more cautious than most. One day Robbie, I and another friend went snorkeling. When I went back up on the shore, I looked over and saw Robbie swimming like a mad woman towards me. It turns out; there was a shark in the water.

While on Kwaj I did get my b-boat license, you could rent a b-boat for ½ day very reasonable. The sunrises and sunsets on the island are the most spectacular thing I have ever seen in my life. I spent thousands of hours sitting at the beach or a bench just watching the beauty of the island and taking it all in. One night a group of us was sitting outside the Pit, we look over and saw a spectacular sight. We were able to see a September harvest moon, which literally left me speechless. The moon was full and it look like it was sitting on the ocean, it was enormous, and I was totally in awe at the beauty of it.

PARADISE

While living on Kwajalein, I saw some people fall in love, some get married while on the island and others just hung out together. As for me, I did not find a serious love while I was there. I do have some fantastic memories though. I cannot think of a better place for romance and memorable times than on a tropical island in paradise, can you? I did have a serious crush on someone from the time I arrived on island, pretty much until I left. All I have to show for it literally is a t-shirt, so in case you are reading this by chance (wink, wink, nudge, nudge, smile, smile just kidding!).

I was able to see some of the missions while I was there. The launching and interceptions of the rockets and to witness firsthand the reason I was given the opportunity to live and work at the test site and what I believe to witness was history in the making.

While sitting at the Pit one night I heard a southern accent. The woman with the accent announced that her name was Teresa Bell, which was a name I recognized right away. Teresa worked in Human Resources and was the one who help those of us moving to Kwajalein. She and I start talking, and soon we became fast friends. Teresa was TDY on Kwaj for a few weeks. I was able to get off work for a day and she, Dan, and I went to Ebeye. Dan who was a firefighter at the time made sure, that Teresa and I would be okay. He brought plenty of Gatorade and water; he was our guide and bodyguard. Teresa does not like water too much, and we decided to take a water taxi back to Kwaj. The water taxi was going fast, and Teresa and I kept saying to each other that if anything did happen Dan would take care of things. He was our hero that day and we knew we were safe. In the meantime, our knuckles were turning white from holding on to the boat because of how fast it was going. During Teresa's visit, we went to the beach several times and to a few events that were going on around the island. Teresa, Dan, Dean, and I flew to Roi for the weekend, what a terrific time that was. Teresa thank you so much, for the surprise care packages you would send me my friend and the beautiful gifts from home. Thank you for your support and encouragement whenever I have needed it, I always know you are just a phone call away.

I have many memories, as I am sure you can imagine, many I have written about already and here are a few more that I will carry with me for the rest of my days. Besides the beauty of the island, I will always remember the people who are in my heart and gave me unforgettable memories to last me a lifetime. Watching the dolphins, flying to Roi Namur, playing pool or darts at the Yuk Club with people who always kept me smiling and were able to teach me a thing or two. Going to the Adult Recreation Center, watching football, and enjoying BBQ's there. The crying bench, sitting on the curb outside the BQ, and people just stopping by to say hi and chat. Experiencing new and different cultural experiences, with the Marshallese people. Two of my most memorable are, the first Christmas I was on Kwajalein, I walk over to the snack bar, as I was leaving the cashier stopped me. I actually did not know her all that well, other than to say hi and talk a little when she would check me out with my food. She gave me a beautiful purse that was handmade, and it had a Marshallese necklace, bracelet, and a pair of earnings in it. She told me she wanted to give them to me, because I always had a smile on my face, and was friendly to everyone no matter what his or her job was or where they were from.

At the hospital, we held clinics for the Marshallese patients occasionally, one my last days of work happen to be on the day we were having the clinic. A group of the patients sang to me in Marshallese and gave me homemade gifts. I had seen them do this for some of my other coworkers, I was very surprised and honored that they did this for me.

Some more of my favorite memories are getting myself in the best physical condition I ever been in. Laughing so hard my side hurt, and knowing if I was sad or upset about something there was someone to listen, who would not judge me, and keep my confidences. Without question, always having a sense of feeling safe and secure, like I had never experienced in my life. When given a commander's coin, from the Range Commander. My daughter Tina, has a full display case of them, and I would tease her, and tell her I wanted one. She would laugh at me and say "Sorry Mom." While on Kwaj, I was both surprised and honored that I recieved one. And of course showing my daughter and saying, "see mom has one too!"

Some of my best memories were also meeting some of the people who were TDY. We had everyone from the Coast Guard, Navy, Marines, Air Force, Army, Australian Air Force Pilots come to the island. As well as defense contractors from Department of Energy, Space X and others.

One of my favorite memories is when my kids, grand-kids, and I met up in Hawaii, even though it rained most of the time. I was sad my son and his family could not make it, but Shawna and her two little ones, Tina, her husband and their 2 kids were able to come. We went to a Luau and The Arizona Memorial at Pearl Harbor, the waterfalls, Diamond Head the Dole plantation and places like that. I will never forget the day my family was heading back to the airport to fly back home. My 16-year-old grandson Jonathon was giving me a very tight hug goodbye and with tears in his eyes, he said, "Grandma, I always knew how much I loved you, but I never knew how much I missed you."

After being on the island for almost two years, my contract had been fullfilled. My supervisor had left several months before, and things were just not the same in my office. There were things going on at home that I felt I needed to leave and attend to but mostly, because I really missed my kids and grandbabies. It was time to go home. I had two Permanente Change of Station (PCS) parties and they were wonderful, yet so very hard. I do not think I have ever cried so many happy/sad tears at the same time in my life. Sad because I knew I was leaving, and this indescribable experience would be ending after two years. Happy because I was going home to my family, and bringing with me memories to last a lifetime.

The most valuable memory I have of Kwajalein is all of the hurt, pain, confusion you have read about in this book leading up to 2005. I was finally able to confront and heal entirely from it, and I owe this all, I truly believe to my time there. Since coming back when faced with something difficult, I use the tools I was able to acquire, the memories that bring such smiles to my heart, and the peace I felt while living there, and bring it home to where I am today. When I returned home, people were always telling me how I had changed, and there was serenity about me, they had never seen before and I was just a different person in many ways.

I hope to go back someday, to the place, that is so close to my heart where my dad is laid to rest and to see those of my Kwaj family who are still living on the island. I would love to visit or who knows; maybe when I finish my degrees I can go back and work there. People have always told me, Kwajalein is shaped is like a boomerang for a reason, people who leave almost always come back!

Photo Gallery

Younger Years

115

My Little Ones

Tina Grown Up

Jeremy Grown Up

Shawna Grown Up

119

Grandmas Sweeties

Paradise AKA Kwajalein

121

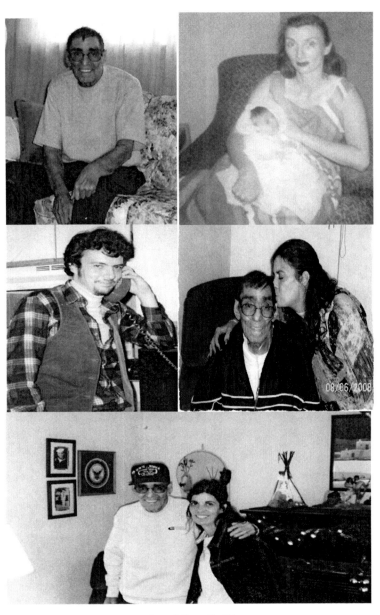

Loved Ones In Heaven

122

Grandma's Angels

I Am So Proud

124

12

Not All Relationships End Bad

Some people do not understand how you can still be friends with someone you were in a romantic relationship with. In my experience, I was unsure myself. Well I am about to tell you it can be done. I was online at a dating site before I came home from overseas and I saw a profile that caught my eye. I usually was not the first to show interest, but this person seem different, and I wanted to see if maybe he was interested, as well. His name was Barry Price.

The first thing, which caught my eye about Barry, was he had been a single dad for many years, and raising his kids was the top priority in his life. Barry was cute and had a terrific sense of humor; he was very down to earth, and there was an honesty about him. He had a terrific sense of humor and honesty about him. We emailed back and forth, and after a few weeks he asked for my phone number. A few minutes later, my phone rang and it was Barry. We were both nervous with our first hello but after a few minutes it seemed like the most natural thing in the world to be talking to each other. Over time, our conversations would keep us up until three or four o'clock in the morning it was exciting and fun. We would drag ourselves to work the next day after our late night talks, but it was so worth it, and I would go to work with a big smile on my face.

After a few months, Barry dropped the "L bomb" as he called it. I was both surprised and happy. He was so sweet, and he sounded just like a shy little boy the first time he told me he loved me. There was complete silence on both ends of the phone lines waiting to hear what my reaction would be. It was certainly a positive one.

Our relationship was progressing extremely well, and within weeks, he booked a flight to come visit. Barry was on an early afternoon flight, so when I got off work my daughter Tina and I headed to the airport. I was excited and could not wait to see him. And when I did see him, I could not stop smiling.

Barry's intelligence certainly impressed me. It was refreshing to be able to carry on a conversation with someone who actually knows what he is talking about and articulates as well as he does. To me it is sexy. He would also explain things to me and if I did not quite understand a subject, he did not make me feel like an idiot. Barry has work many years for a major international corporation. In his job he repairs, and programs computer systems for both commercial and government aircraft. I have dated people whose occupations range from construction workers, corporate professionals, doctors, police officers, firefighters, and all types in-between but he was different.

During his visit, Barry made dinner for Tina's family and me. He cooked us a homemade chicken and noodle dinner which was delicious. And he even made the noodles from scratch! We were all quite impressed. Barry and I spent the next six days in a world of our own it was fantastic, except when I almost burn down the apartment, and sent my dog flying through the air, but that is another story. However, even that did not distract us from our time together. I baked a few dozen peanut butter cookies for him, he was so sweet and genuinely appreciated them, and I have never in my life, met a man who loves his peanut butter quite like he does, it was just one more endearing quality about him.

I flew to Ohio a few months later after Barry's visit, and we had an outstanding time. In the spring and summer Barry sails his boat, and in the winter he is an avid snowboarder. While I was up visiting one evening we went on a moonlight sail, and it was amazing. While on my visit, I met Barry's beautiful daughters and granddaughter and we got along immediately. Barry, lives in a beautiful log cabin house right by a lake, which I instantly fell in love with it.

Barry drove me to see my dad while I was visiting. It was a three-hour drive, and I had not seen my dad for many years and I was extremely nervous. Barry, my dad, my stepmother, and I had a fantastic time during our visit. My dad help to create the first magnetic core memory, it was the very first nonvolatile memory for a computer, and Barry actually had one at his house, which in itself it is amazing and the two of them had a great time comparing notes. I was very grateful that we were all able to have spent this time together.

Barry was kind, considerate, as well as romantic; he would send me gifts in the mail and was constantly surprising me. For my birthday, he sent me a gift certificate for a day at the spa, which was awesome. For Valentine's Day, Barry surprised me with a huge bouquet of flowers. He knew how much I had loved my time living on Kwajalein, and he had the florist coordinate my bouquet with the types of flowers you would find there. It was so thoughtful and touching.

We decided that we were going to make plans to move in together, and hoped to get married eventually. We made plans for me to move to Ohio and starting talking about future wedding plans as well.

I sent out resumes throughout the area where Barry lived but had no response. A few months before I was suppose to move up to Ohio, I was offered a contract position for The Department of Energy in Albuquerque. I did not know what to do. If I took the job then Barry and I would be farther apart by miles, but I also knew there was no way, I was going to move in with him without a job secured. He reassured me that he could handle everything financially until I could get a job. I knew he could, but I just did not feel right about having him support me, and was not comfortable moving there until I was sure I could pull my own weight.

When offered the job in Albuquerque, Barry told me he knew it was an opportunity that I should not pass up, and we would figure everything out one way or the other. With reluctance, I decided to go back to New Mexico.

Within a short time of accepting the position, I felt Barry was becoming distant, and it was becoming more obvious with each passing day. My heart knew that he did not want to be with me anymore, and that is exactly what happened. The hardest part was there was a distance between us and not just by the miles that separated us. I believed I knew the answer, yet I had not heard the words out of his mouth. I figured he had his reasons but it was still very painful, that he just lost contact with me.

Months had passed, and I decided to send Barry an email to let him know about my daughters mother-in-law who passed away. Barry had always been a great comfort to me, and I knew from our past that he was always someone I could talk to. I was hoping that he was still the same person as before, and he was. We started keeping in touch again through emails and phone calls occasionally. For awhile, neither one of us talked about our breakup. Then one day he explained to me what had happend. After we discussed the break-up he told me how badly he felt that things had ended the way they did.

I believe neither one of us wanted things to end the way they did, but it does happen. Barry and I have remained great friends. He is one of the few men in my life, which I had a serious relationship with, and I am able to keep all the good memories, smiles and laughter in my heart without them being tarnish by a lot of pain and sorrow. Although I was very upset and hurt when we broke up, it was a different kind of pain than what I had experienced before. It was not a malicious hurt, or a physical hurt, but we were just two people not meant to be together at that time.

13

Daddy's Girl

In early August of 2008, I recieved a phone, telling me that my dad had been released from the hospital, and he was now going to be under hospice care. I was also told if I wanted to say good-bye to him, that this would be the time to do so. This news totally shocked me, I was in no way prepared and had no idea my dad was even sick. I talked to my supervisor to let her know the situation, and ask for some time off.

At the time, I was working for New Mexico VA Healthcare Systems and they were extremely compassionate and understanding of my situation. My emotions were scatter all over the place. My dad and I, within the past few years of this call, had finally restablished a close relationship with each other. I flew to Ohio within a couple of days of this call. My daughter and sister Nita pick me up at the airport. When we got to dad's house, I walk in the door, and ran over and gave my dad a hug and proceeded to sit on his oxygen line. My brother while teasing me was saying, "Great, Michele, you haven't been in the room 10 seconds yet, and you're already killing dad!" Dad thought this was funny as well.

I stayed in Ohio for six days and it was an extremely emotional visit. When it came time to say goodbye, I of course thought this would be the last time I would ever see my dad. I flew home crying while my heart was breaking. Dad knew how sick he was, so he wanted to say goodbye to us kids when he was still himself, and not "on his deathbed' as he put it.

I went back to work and called my stepmother and dad several times a day, and within three days of returning home, I received a call from the hospice nurse. He told me that my dad had taken a turn for the worse. I ask him if he thought I should come back, and he said yes. I informed my supervisor, booked a flight, and headed back to Ohio.

When I arrived my dad was extremely surprised to see me apparently, he had no idea I was coming back. He then looked at me, smiled and told me how happy he was I was there. He also told me that he did not want anyone else to have to see him go through this.

While I was there, we spent countless hours talking and watching TV. He answered all my questions I had wanted to ask him my whole life. He told me he did not hate my mom, which I actually thought he had; he explained to me, why I had not been a part of his life for many years, like my siblings had been.

I developed a close realtionship with my dad's hospice team while I was there. His team consisted of his doctor, nurses, caseworker, and chaplain. They were all terrific, patient and kind to dad, my stepmother, and me.

I was grateful to my step-mother for allowing me to be there. This was only the third time, I had been to my dad's house in over 35 years and only a handful of times I had seen him in person. Dad and I had been talking on the phone every week, for three years before this happened, and we worked so hard to get to the point we were finally at.

My dad had many rough and sleepless nights; he would get up, walk around the house with his little walker, sit up, walk, lie down, and back up again. Since he had not been sleeping, the doctor and nurses had been trying different medications. One of the medications was an antipsychotic drug. Dad had taken only one pill and said that he felt like a zombie. He kept telling me, "Sweetheart, I don't like this, I really don't like this," and then he kept apologizing for being so much trouble. I reassured him that it would be okay and he in no way was trouble at all. I called his hospice nurse immediately, and I asked her to please take my dad off the medication and to prescribe something else. I knew they were trying to help him sleep, but he appeared to be having an adverse reaction, and he hated it. I looked over at my dad, and he smiled and mouthed the words to me, "I love you honey."

SHATTERED PIECES, LOVING HEART

His hospice nurse came to the house the next morning and brought what hospice calls a comfort pack, which includes morphine and other medications. She went over the instructions with my stepmother and me. When the seal of the comfort pack is broken, the law requires that a nurse is present, and the caregiver must be able to account for every dose of the medication that has been given. The morphine seemed to be helping my dad, it was a small dose, but when given with an anti-anxiety pill, the combination of the two helped him to rest a little better.

I suggested we buy an iPod for Dad, he really seem to enjoyed listening to mine. I download all his favorite Spanish music along with other types that I knew he loved. I also found a CD to download with acoustic guitar and ocean waves in the background. Dad told me he loved it and when I would check on him throughout the night, he seemed to be resting a little better with his music playing.

My daddy and I spent hours talking about when he was in the military. One day I look at him and said "Daddy, I would love to record some of these things you're telling me about." Next thing I knew he was sending my stepmother and me to go buy a video camera for me, and I started recording videos of him.

One day while laying beside him on his bed, we started talking and sharing things we had never discussed before. I laid my head on my daddy's chest, just like i had when I was a little girl. We both had been crying, and he brush the hair from my cheek, and wiped my tears away. We spent the next several hours just being there together. My dad and I were able to say what we needed to during this time and to put closure on our past. It was an extraordinary time for the both of us, and one of the greatest gifts I have ever received.

My step mom had gone out to run errands one afternoon, and when she returned, Dad handed me a gift bag. Inside was a box, with a beautiful sapphire necklace. I was very surprised, he looked at me and said, "I just wanted to get you something, and I love you sweetheart."

I called Dad's hospice caseworker Pam one day, and I asked if she could help me to get some infomation that I needed. She called me back immediately and showed up at the house with some paperwork, along with a list of phone numbers I had asked her to bring to me.

My dad was in the South Pacific in the 1940s, throughout my childhood whenever he would talk about his time there, he always told me how much he loved it. As much as I hated to bring the subject up, I was curious as to what his wishes were once he was gone. I knew one of his wishes was cremation, and when I brought the subject up about his final resting place. My stepmother told me his burial would be at the military cemetery in Ohio. I looked at my dad and asked him "Daddy what would you think of having a Navy funeral, with full military honors, and spend eternity on the water by Kwajalein in the South Pacific?" I told him, I hoped it was okay that I had been in touch with the Navy and had the paperwork. If this is what he wanted then we would go over the paper work together and make it happen. He got a huge smile on his face, and with tears in his eyes he said, "Let's do it," And we did.

I needed to get back to Albuquerque and take care of a few things. I had been in Ohio for 5 ½ weeks, so I booked a flight for Wednesday September 3rd. I did not want to leave, but we knew it was time. While I was waiting to go to the airport, we taped one last video, took some pictures and then my cell phone rang. The caller was the brother of Dean Gross. Dean was one of my best friends from Kwajalein his brother had called to let me know Dean had died. I had just talked to Dean the night before, he had been calling me every few nights to see how my dad was doing. It was an enormous shock. Dean was only 36 years old and he and I were very close. Dean's parents and I had talked on the phone several times prior to recieving this phone call. I was very grateful to his family for letting me know of his passing.

It was time for me to leave for the airport, my dad and I said our goodbyes. I turned around and looked at my daddy one last time before walking out the door. With tears streaming down my face, and through his tears he gave me a smile and a big thumbs up.

On September 9th, six days after I left Ohio, I recieved a phone call saying my dad was not doing well. During this call when the phone was held up to my Dad, one minute he would be yelling at me as to why I was not there with him, and the next he would be yelling that he did not want me to come back and for me to stay away. I knew he was slipping fast. I was not able to get a flight out the next day, but I was able to book one for 7:30 am on September 11th. At 6:00 am, while waiting for my friend Barb to take me to the airport, I recived a called that my dad had died. I had just really found my dad again only a few years before, and now he was gone. I know how lucky I was, that he wanted me there with him for his final weeks, and he and I were able to have spent some wonderful time together, but my heart was shattered.

My eldest daughter Tina and her Grandpa had a very special and close relationship. I wanted to have a service for my dad, so Tina and I put together, a Memorial Celebration of his life.Tina was able to reserve the oldest chapel at Fort Sill for the service. The Chaplain was Spanish, and was also active-duty military, it was perfect and so fitting for my dad. Tina, I know your grandpa was smiling and saying, "That's my girl."

My dad's service was held on Oct 11, which would give any family members who wanted to attend the opportunity to do so if they needed to travel. Tina and I put together a PowerPoint presentaion, and I picked out and played music that I knew my dad loved. We had family from Ohio, Texas and Florida come for the service. John flew in from Utah to Albuquerque, and he I drove to Oklahoma.

I tried to put into words the best I could and how I felt

as my daughter Tina stood beside me, and held me up to read this on the day of his service.

Daddy, I am really not very articulate when I write, but there are a few things, I need to say to you. I know you already know them, as I read this to you before I left you a few days ago, but I had to tell you one last time. You have been such a gift in my life, what a privilege it has been to be able to call myself your daughter. Throughout our time together, there have been many mountains, valleys, difficulties and of course my "scatterbrain" years, but our love never wavered. The legacy dad you left to me is priceless, and I cannot even put into words, but I will try. You taught me respect, honor, morals, values, love, sensitivity, pride, caring, and trust. You show me always through example how to be a person of my word and be true to myself. I remember you always telling me during my "scatterbrain" years "When we leave this earth Michele, the only thing we take with us is our integrity, so always keep it intact." As I told you, the three most important things you ever said to me were, "I love you, I am proud of you, and I was your girl." You smiled and told me, "Well honey, I do, I am, and you are!" I waited my entire life to hear how proud you are of me. You never gave up on me and always had faith in me even when I did not have it in myself. Dad, all of the things you taught me I was able to pass down to my three children Tina, Jeremy and Shawna. I believe Tina aquired her love of law enforcement and the miltary, Jeremy's knowledge of engineering, and Shawna's, love for medicine all came from you. In addition, all three of them got their no nonsense attitude from you, that is for sure! Daddy, you, and I were able as you said to have closure in our relationship, talk through everything, and come full circle. We laughed and cried together as I laid in your bed, with my head on your chest and you brushed the hair from my cheek just like when I was a little girl. We cried many tears together, both of sorrow for the loss of time between us, and of happiness that we had finally found each other again. We talked about our lives, and we were able to answer all of the questions we had for each other. What a blessing this was to me, and I thank you! I made you a promise, which I will try the best of my ability to keep, and finish the project you entrusted to me that we had started together and I will finish in your honor and get the message to everyone. Daddy you and I were able to share a special bond, as you always said, because of the time we had spent on Kwajalein in the South Pacific. You were so excited for me, that I was able to experience the place that you had been to so many years ago. And, I am honored to have been able to arrange my final gift to you where God and the angels are waiting for you and you will be among the stars, the beautiful sunrises, sunsets, the crystal clear water, and the peaceful tranquility of the ocean waves. I cannot even come close to finding the words to say good-bye to you, but I know that you know, just as you know that I know, that our love for each other is beyond this physical earth. I will see you again Daddy, when it is my time to join you, and we can watch our beautiful sunrises, and sunsets together. I thank you for bringing me into this world and for making me a better person by having been your daughter. With love, respect, admiration, hugs, kisses and a big thumbs up. Always and forever, Your loving daughter, Michele

14

Earthy Crunchy

I met my friend Barbara Metcalf, 23 years ago through our mutual friend Pam. We would see each other on occasion throughout the years until Pam's was diagnosed with terminal cancer. Barb and I started spending more time together and became friends.

When Pam passed away in 1999, Barb and I started spending a lot of time together. Barb and her husband owned a home business, and she hired me to help her with the accounting and administrative work that needed to be done. Within a short time. we became the best of friends.

Barb was diagnosed with insulin dependent diabetes at the young age of 11. The doctors said she was a brittle diabetic, which meant her blood sugar levels were unpredictable and would go from very low to very high. When Barb and I first met, she was very active and she seemed to have her health under control. After she and her husband were divorced, I watched as Barb's health started to slowly deteriorate. Barb always claimed it was not because of the divorce, but in my opinion, I think the divorce did play at least a small part in her declining health.

While I was overseas, Barb told me that she was homeless and had been sleeping in her car. This was a woman who had a beautiful house and a home business, who vacationed in Europe and Hawaii, and now she was homeless? About two years ago, things started started to go downhill in Barb's life. She had no real stability and was sleeping from couch to couch at different friends' houses. During this time, Barb and her family were estranged, and Barb's moods seemed to be more erratic.

January of 2009, a woman named Bea offered Barb a place to stay. Barb would call me on a daily basis, upset because of the situation at the house. She did not want to live there but she had no where else to go. I told Barb, she was always welcome to come and stay with me here in Oklahoma, but her son was still in high school living with his dad, and she didn't want to leave him.

Barb told me that her family had been making accusations of mental instability, and they talked about "putting her in a psychiatric hospital and just leaving her there." She was terrified, and convinced that this was going to happen. As her health was getting worse, she was more afraid of what she thought her family was planning to do, than what was going on with her health. She would tell me, that her family had meetings with social workers at her parent's house and she did not know what to do. To be honest, I was not sure what to think about the situation but what I did know was my friend was extremely frightened, and thought she was in trouble.

Besides her living arrangements, Barb was also dealing with her father's serious health condition. Her dad was admitted into a home hospice facility. Barb seemed to think this was a personal attack on her father, as well as herself. She was very close to him and in denial of his condition. She would tell me that she knew he was going to improve. I explained to her a few times what hospice was about. She knew the concept, but I believe it was just too hard and painful for her to accept what was going on with her dad.

There were times when my friend did not take responsibility for her actions, or it seemed it was always someone elses fault. When she finally realized maybe it was not, many people felt it was too late and they pushed her out of their lives. It's one thing if an acquaintance does this, but when family and close friends do, to me it's just not right. There were situations throughout the years as well, that tested my friendship with Barb, but I believe that family and true friends should talk it out.

When Barb's health starting plummeting last year she called me, and we discuss what her options were. She said what made sense to her was for me to be her Medical Power of Attorney (MPOA) and General Power of Attorney

(GPOA). I agreed and downloaded all the paperwork. We filled the paperwork out over the phone line-by-line, systematically. We reviewed the paperwork over the phone several times, until I felt comfortable enough, knowing she understood what she was signing. I was not doubting her intelligence by any means, I just wanted to make sure that her emotional family issues were not clouding her judgment on asking me to do this. She notarized the paperwork and faxed it to me, and I forwarded it on to her doctors.

Within one day of finalizing Barb's paperwork, she called me, confused and clearing in a lot of pain. I asked her to hand the phone to the lady whose house she was at. This lady, Bea, was screaming in the phone at me, "Well I don't know if I should call an ambulance. Barbara is not breathing right or making any sense. She is really making me mad, and I want her out of my house now!" I yelled at Bea to call the ambulance. She gave the phone back to Barb, who by this time could not even to talk to me and I stayed on the line until the ambulance arrived. To make matters even worse, while Barb was being transported to the hospital, Bea was calling Barb's elderly mother and myself, saying obnoxious and hateful things about Barb. Bea told me, "When Barb gets out of the hospital, she is not to come back here." I told her a few 'choice words' and hung up.

Barb was admitted into the hospital and it was determined she had a serious infection in her foot. When a person has diabetes to the severity of her condition wounds can be dangerous. Barb had become uncooperative shortly after her admission to the hospital. She had been acting mean and nasty, not only to the hosptial staff but to me as well. I admit, it tested my patience to the limits this time. But within a day or two, I realized her anger and frustration was not only from probably being afraid of what was happening to her health, but the toxic build up in her body as well, due to her diabetes. I felt guilty for being angry for those two days, but I was frustrated and very tired.

A few days later my phone rang and it was Barb's doctor. He was ready to begin Barb's procedure, and before she allowed them to put her under anesthesia she begged him to call me and apologize for her for the way she had been treating me. I thanked her doctor for calling me and asked him to reassure her that it was okay, and I loved her and not to worry.

Barb's surgery went well, and after she was released from the hospital, she was admitted to a nursing facility to have IV antibiotics infused. Shortly after her admission to the facility, Barb's kidneys started shutting down, and she was gaining weight at an alarming rate. When the nurses or I tried to get ahold of Barb's doctors no one would return our calls. I was making arrangements to head out to Albuquerque, when the on-call doctor from the facility called me. He said he had been trying to get ahold Barb's specialists as well. He was going to transport Barb to the hospital as a direct admission and ask another specialist to consult on her case.

SHATTERED PIECES, LOVING HEART

Within hours of her admission into the hospital, Barb started emergency dialysis that began to remove the toxins from her body. Barb could not even move her legs due to the fluid buildup by this time. The nurses told me they removed 65 pounds of fluid after the first few days. Barb underwent dialysis everyday, until they were able to get her condition under control, and then she was scheduled for every other day.

Barb was in a coma-like state the first few days she was in the hospital. I called the nurses' station every few hours to keep track of her condition. The hospital called me at one point to get permission to give her a blood transfusion, and this seemed to help. Once Barb was stable, they sent her back to the facility to finish her rehabilitation.

The nurses told me Barb had become a different person when she came back to the facility and I could tell quite a difference as well. Barb stayed in rehab for a total of three months, and then moved into an efficiency apartment. Things seem to be looking up for her, she said the doctors even told her that she would be able to avoid dialysis and take a break from it for a year or two.

On May 4th, my phone rang and Barb was just beside herself. Her beloved father had passed away. She always told me there were two people she knew that she could always count on for anything and she trusted with her life. One was her father and I was the other. I felt honored, but at the same time, I was tremendously sad. I hated the fact that she had to come to me, a friend, to make her final decisions and not someone in her family.

Barb and her children were estranged. She used to tell me she never understood why it had happened. She told me she would never get over the hurt and pain it caused her. Her youngest son she did have some contact with, but not with her two oldest. I can not even begin to imagine if my kids were not in my life. From what my friend had told me over the years, there were many issues that were unresolved between she and her family. Over the past year, Barb told me that she and her brother were mending their relationship and she was very grateful and happy about that. She also started going to church with her mother, and that meant the world to her. Barb said that she and her mom were more like acquaintances, and things were on a platonic level, but it was a start and they could work from there. I used to tell Barb that I knew that even if they were not close, her mom and her kids loved her. I may not have always understood the dynamics of their situation, but I do know her kids and her mom, and I believe I know their hearts.

When she asked me to be her MPOA and GPOA, my hope was to be able to reunite Barb with her family. I told her that was what I had hoped for, and she of course wanted the same thing. Neither one of us ever gave up that hope. I felt like I was in the middle a lot of times between Barb, her kids and her mom because I could see both sides. I have known Barb's kids for many years, and

SHATTERED PIECES, LOVING HEART

I love them like they are a part of my family. They have always treated me with nothing but respect and love. And since I have known Barb's mom, she has done the same.

Barb needed to have another surgery on her foot, because her doctor felt her infection had gone into her bone again, only this time deeper. The night before her surgery, Barb fell in the parking lot of her apartment complex and hit her head on the cement. Barb had lost her balance and fallen down a few times prior to this happening; she said it was because of the neuropathy caused by the diabetes. With this fall thought she lost consciousness and someone from the apartments called an ambulance. In the evening when I called Barb, she told me about her fall and since she was scheduled for surgery on her foot the next day, the hospital went ahead and admitted her. While talking to her on the phone, she kept telling me how much pain she was in from falling.

The doctors went ahead and operated the following day as scheduled on her foot. For a few days, she seemed to be doing okay. On Monday August 23rd, Barb called me hysterically and told me that they were going to be putting a port and a catheter in her because they wanted to start dialysis right away. She said they would be taking her to surgery within the hour. This phone call was different, Barb was frightened and crying. She kept telling me she did not want the surgery. She knew she needed to have it done even though she did not want to. I had never heard such fear in my friend's voice before. Barb reluctantly agreed to the surgery.

EARTHY CRUNCHY

After getting out my first day of class that afternoon, I called Barb's cell phone and her hospital room to check on her. There was no answer on either phone, so after several tries, I called the nurses' station to see what was going on. The nurse told me they had moved Barb to the ICU unit before surgey had even been completed. The nurse said during surgery Barb had a PEA (*pulseless electrical activity*) her heart rhythm was not producing a pulse and she went into cardiac arrest and was put on a respirator.

The hospital staff was supposed to call me because I had her MPOA. Instead, they called someone else that was on her medical record from years before. I was very angry; I had no idea what had been going on with my friend's condition this whole time until I called to check up on her. I started arranging to head out to New Mexico, and I called the hospital a few more times that night. The nurses reassured me that I could wait a few days to go to Albuquerque because Barb was doing better. It's not that I did not want to go, but I had just started classes at the University on that day, and if Barb was stable, I thought it would be okay to wait until the weekend.

The following day, which was Tuesday, the doctor was going to try and wean her off the respirator, and by Wednesday they were sucessful. Barb was still extremely lethargic but her condition was now more stable. On Thursday August 26th, Barb was moved out of ICU and into a less critical ward. She was still lethargic and what the nurses described to me as *loopy*.

SHATTERED PIECES, LOVING HEART

Later that evening, when I called the nurses' station, the nurse on duty told me that I did not need to be calling every few hours. She said Barb was stable, and if anything changed they would notifiy me. I called back anyway, and around 10 pm, talked to a different nurse. She told me Barb was still lethargic and discussed Barb's most recent lab results with me. She also said that they were waiting on the results of a CT scan and chest-xray the doctor had just ordered. Barb's nurse was not alarmed at all and reassured me there was no change in Barb's condition.

Within a few hours, my phone rang and it was Barb's nurse and she told me that they did not think Barb would live through the night. I called Barb's eldest daughter right away, and told her what the nurse had told me, and if she and her family wanted to say good-bye, they needed to get to the hospital as soon as they could.

Twenty minutes later, on the morning of August 27, 2010, the charge nurse called to inform me that my beloved friend had died. I called Barb's daughter back to tell her that her mom had just passed away. My heart was sad, once again I had lost yet another person in my life who I loved.

I booked a flight to Albuquerque and I started calling people to let them know what had happened. I called one of Barb's friends, to let her know of Barb's passing. I knew from our conversations that Barb had only known her for a few months. I told her friend that I was flying in to Albuquerque that night and would be going to the hospital to pick up Barb's truck keys and her cell phone. The woman told me that Barb had given her the truck, her keys and cell phone a few days before. The timeline just did not match in my opinion, because the nursing staff had been telling me that Barb had been lethargic and 'loopy,' and had not been cognizant of things going on when this took place. Her friend did not seem to pleased with me at first when I told her I would be in Albuquerque and that we needed to meet up the next day so I could get Barb's belongings.

Tina and Sam took me to the airport that evening, and Barb's kids met me when I arrived in Albuquerque. Barb's mom was very gracious and invited me to stay in her home while I was there. The next day, Barb's daughters and I went to pick up Barb's belongings and take care of business that needed to be done. When Barb's family started arriving from out of town, I decided to get a hotel room and spend some time by myself.

Since I had arrived in Albuquerque, there were some things going on that I knew Barb would be very upset about. Without going into detail, I decided not to attend Barb's memorial service. It was an extremely hard and painful decision for me to make. However, I loved and respected my friend enough to stand by my decision, and to honor her requests the best I could.

Barb's three kids stopped by the hotel to say goodbye to me, and her youngest daughter drove me to the airport. I went home exhausted, overwhelmed, and sad. This is the letter, I had written to Barb and planned to read at her memorial service, but instead I sent it to the mortuary to post on the site of her obituary.

Barb, we were friends for over 20 years and best of friends for ten of those. I miss you more than words can even begin to say. We talked every day at least once a day. When the world was giving us a hard time, we always knew we had each other to lean on. Your heart was big, open and loving to the world and people you touched ,who would appreciate you for who you were. Your passion for learning and teaching went beyond the ordinary. Your talent for helping others, especially with the literacy program and your special education kids was amazing. My heart is so sad, with the void of not hearing your laughter or knowing we will never have any more of our great times or adventures. Even the few times we did not see eye-to-eye on things, our friendship always remained intact. And we cannot forget the donuts! Knowing we will not be able to talk about our day, our families, dreams, fears, hopes, the pain we felt at times makes my heart sad. My prayers are with you, I know you are now up in heaven, no longer in pain, with the the Lord, the angels, your beloved dad, our friend Pam, your best friends Karen and Janey and all of those who left before us. I know they were all there to meet you four days ago with open arms, and their love surrounding you. I miss you my friend! Love, hugs and prayers, always, Mik

15

And Now

There were times when some people used to give me a hard time from when I gave birth to my first child at 18, until my last at 21. They would say hurtful things to me such as, "How could I bring a child into the world being single" or "How dare I have another child at 19 and again at 21." Well, I am extremely lucky because, not only were my children always a gift from God, but a year after I had Shawna at the age of 22 years old I given a diagnosis of cancer for the first time and underwent a complete hysterectomy. In time, I forgave those people for the things they said, but I never forgot the way those words made me feel.

Throughout the years, the very same people who were so hurtful to me, watched how my kids, excelled in school, and all of their accomplishments from a very young age, to where they are today. These people started taking back their words and even in some cases apologizing for their painful and disparaging comments about me. Some of their comments would then be "I wish my kids were like yours?" "How did you raise such great kids?" I will not go into detail about some of the choices their kids made. But I do believe people should think twice about making judgment calls or trying to set others up to fail before they even get started, because you never know how life can turn out in your own backyard.

Tina was very young when she had her first child. She dropped out of high school, earned her GED and went to work right away. She has worked her entire life and would never accept any assistace from the state. She used to tell me "Mom, they can give the help, to someone who needs it, because I am capable of working." Tina has earned three college degrees, including a Master's in Psychology and each degree she has graduated with honors. Tina spent eight years in the military and has held a job as a federal police officer for the past ten years. My daughter has a terrific husband, Sam. Sam is a very loving, funny, smart, handsome man, and my daughter is the happiest I have ever seen her. Tina has two kids of her own. Jonathon, who will graduate from college with a bachelor's degree in economics this May, has attended college on full academic scholarships. After graduation, he plans to pursue his master's degree, and then his PhD. Tina's youngest daughter, Carrie, works as a veterinary technician and will be starting college in the spring. Both of her kids are loving and wonderful young adults. When Tina remarried, her husband had seven kids of his own so she became mother of nine children. Two of the boys live with Tina and Sam, and I absolutly adore them. They are just as much a part of my heart, as all my other grandkids. Tina is loving and kind, and is always there for the people she loves. She is a remarkable example of what you can accomplish, no matter what life hands you, with grace, class, determination and compassion.

In September of 1975, I gave birth to a beautiful eight-pound one-ounce little boy, Jeremy Michael. He was my easiest delivery and my quietest newborn. Jeremy was so cute and entertaining to watch as he grew up; he was sensitive and highly intelligent. Jeremy tried to set up his kindergarten teacher and me on a date, and I thought he was so darn cute in doing this. He would look at me with that cute little impish smile of his and say, "Well mommy somebody needs to love you, besides us kids. We love you lots and lots, but you need someone to take care of you like you do us." It melted my heart. As I watched this little boy grown into a young man, he went through all of the crazy, normal teenage stuff, but nothing to out of the ordinary as far as teenage angst. He was always, so sweet and considerate of his mom. When he was a teenager, he and his friend snuck out of the house one night. I woke up in a panic not knowing where he was, and on the table in clear sight in large letters was a note, which said, "Mom, I snuck out and I did not want you to worry. We are over sitting on top of the roof at Sandia High School just hanging out. I knew how upset you would get if you could not find me, and you would go into a major meltdown. I hope I am not in too much trouble, Love Jeremy." Now how can you get mad at that? I could not. Jeremy started karate as a little boy and he excelled in it like everything he has done. My son has always been highly intelligent, both in working with technology and on an academic level. His teachers would tell me, "He is a brilliant young man but gets bored easily, so keep his mind stimulated and occupied." When I got my first computer back in the 1980s, it was Jeremy who sat down and taught me how to use it. Jeremy has also spent time in the Air Force. He now works for a global corporation as an Advanced Response Direct Analyst. My son is married to his devoted and loving wife Cindy, and they have a beautiful, smart, and loving son Xavier. Xavier just learned to play chess and made the honor roll at his school, and he is only in the first grade! My son Jeremy has been successful in all aspects of his life and he is an incredible son, man, husband, and father.

My Shawna is my baby, and even though she used to get mad me when she was young for calling her that, she always will be. Shawna was on drill team as well as the swim team in high school, and she was my social butterfly throughout junior high and high school. Shawna has always been sweet and loving, but is also a no nonsense kind of girl, she tells it like it is, and always backs up what she puts out there. Shawna is married to the love of her life, her husband John. He works full time as a computer programmer and also owns his own custom Harley Davidson motorcycle shop in Fort Worth, Texas. My son-in-law turns out the most beautiful bikes I have ever seen. They have been featured on TV and magazines around the world, with my daughter on a few of the covers. John is a loving, caring, good man, who is a wonderful husband to my baby girl and an incredible dad to my grandkids. Shawna is a wonderful mother to her two kids Colette and Brody. Colette is brilliant and beautiful, and she is in the National Junior Honor Society, is a member of Speech Club, and is also a cheerleader. Colette also has been playing the violin for four years and is the vice-president of her orchestra class at school as well. All of Colette's classes are Pre-AP honor classes, She is also in a youth group through her church, and a wonderful young person. Shawna's son Brody is not only as cute as can be, but wise beyond his 6 years, he is already learning advanced math, and is reading, and he is only in kindergarten. Brody also recently started learning to play the violin and is following in his sister's footsteps in the musical world. Shawna works full time and just recieved her certification as an Emergency Medical Technician, and she has recently been accepted into the Paramedic Training Program at one of the top trauma hospitals in the nation. My daughter has achieved her success in her life with love, class, and determination.

As for me, I graduated from Pima Medical Institute back in 1986, which actually was the stepping-stone for my love of working in the medical field. I have continued with my education throughout my life off and on. I am currently attending school full time, finishing my bachelor's degree in psychology and hope to obtain my Master of Social Work, with a concentration in Pediatric Hospice. I have volunteered throughout the years with hospice, the mental health community, woman's shelters, homeless shelters, and the American Cancer Society. I have worked in the medical field, for many years. I hold two security clearances, and have worked contract for The Department of Defense and The Department of Energy through various positions. I have also held a position as a federal government employee. I have worked overseas and been able to experience places one can only dream about, and I am a two-time cancer survivor. Most importantly, I have been blessed with an extraordinary family and fantastic friends. I think that very frightened four-year-old little girl, lying in her bed alone, has come a long way. I also believe with all my heart, through the Grace of God, and all the love I have received throughout my lifetime, and that I have been able to give to others, that the *Shattered Pieces of my life came together, as a result of a having a Loving Heart.*

Acknowledgments

I would like say thank my three children, Tina, Jeremy and Shawna, who believed and trusted in me enough to share our lives, while knowing I would try my best to do it with honesty, intregrity, sensitivity and love. Tina for helping me to pick a title for this book and helping me edit the contents in the beginning. Shawna, for sharing pictures, and giving me ideas while helping me to visualize my concepts, and Jeremy for all his patience, insight, and suggestions especially the last few weeks. In addition, to all three of you, thank you for not thinking your mom was *too crazy* for wanting to write this book the first place. You have been a constant encouragement from when I first came up with the idea, until its completion.

Thank you to Jonathon, Carrie, Xavier, Brody, and Colette my beautiful grandchildren, for telling me "Sure Grandma you can use our names in your book." For always loving me and allowing me to love, you back. I would like to add a special thank you to Colette for taking the picture I had for the cover of the book, and *"doing your thing,"* you made it amazing for your Grandma.

Thank you Brian D. Lange, who is not only is my business manager, but one of my closest, dearest, and trusted friends. You gave me the encouragement and confidence in myself to move forward, with the idea of putting my life on paper. You also gave me a kick in the rear when needed as well. Your faith in me has been invaluable at moments when doubting myself, not only while working on the book, but on a personal level as well. And one more thing Brian, Whatever! (Smile!!)

Thank you to my sisters, Laura who made sure I had the pictures I needed right away, which were in my inbox within hours of asking for them. Judy, who kept her bug' laughing and smiling through the tears when I would hit a wall while trying to get this on paper. Dee for your love, encouragement and prayers since I first came up with the idea for writing this book. Maria for your enthusiasm and the support that you always give me. And of course Nita, for your cute reaction of "oh no" when I told you about writing it. I love you all!

Thank you to Dian Kaehele, who has been my friend for over 40 years. You have been a true friend in every sense of the word since we were giggling young girls. You gave me a home when no else seem to want me as a teenager and rescued me when I needed a friend. Had it not been for you in my life, I am not sure where I might have ended up. You loved me no matter what, and have always been on my side! In addition, we cannot forget all the wonderful times we had as well! I love you my friend!

Thank you CB my first supervisor on Kwajalein, your friendship and guidance was invaluable to me. You helped me to find my way back to the Catholic Church, and words cannot convey my gratitude. Had it had not been for you, I would never have been able to experience, both professionally and personally, the phenomenal experience I had from the moment my plane touched down on Kwajalein, and I would not have been able to write this book. It was an honor to have been a part of your team and to call you my friend.

Robbie, you not only shared with me during those amazing two years while on Kwajalein the good times, but also helped me to heal from a lot of my pain that I brought with me. You have been so excited and encouraged me throughout this project, and I am truly grateful. Thank you, for sending me the picture of our "Crying Bench," and telling me "Here you go Albercookie, do with it what you will." I love you girl! Thanks Boston!

Barry, thank you for all of your encouragement and input, and for letting me know that if I needed any help, you would be there for me while working on this project. You kept me smiling and laughing through your messages. And thank you so much for designing and building my website for me.

Thank you Father John Sheehan, without your guidance, sense of humor and spiritual help I certainly would not have been able to do this.

A special thank you to Bridget H., my wonderful Author Representative from Outskirts Press, who went above and beyond to help me get my book into print. Your kindness, sense of humor, companssion and professionalism were certainly instrumental in helping me to fullfill my dream, and I am very grateful to you.

Thank you, Marion R. I am forever grateful to you for helping me to open my heart and head during our talks. You gave me the tools that I needed to finally be angry when I should, to forgive when necessary and to heal completely. By accomplishing this, it gave me the courage to be able to share with other by writing this book.

There are many more individuals who I have not mentioned by name, but I would like to thank you all for being a part of my life and for allowing me to write about my journey.

LaVergne, TN USA
17 February 2011
216835LV00010B/21/P